P9-EKX-331

Premier World Atlas, © Copyright 1989 by Rand McNally & Company,
R.L. 88-S-147

Enchantment of the World

GREENLAND

By Emilie U. Lepthien

Consultants for Greenland: Claus Andreasen, Director, The Museum of Greenland, Nuuk
H. Peter Krosby, Ph.D., Professor of History, State University of New York, Albany, New York

Consultant for Reading: Robert L. Hillerich, Ph.D., Bowling Green State University, Bowling Green, Ohio

 CHILDRENS PRESS ®

CHICAGO

Dog sleds are used for hunting above the Arctic Circle.
Even in summer, icebergs float in the fjords (opposite page).

To Fran Dyra, editorial director, for advice, friendship, and encouragement

Library of Congress Cataloging-in-Publication Data

Lepthien, Emilie U. (Emilie Utteg)
    Greenland / by Emilie U. Lepthien.
    p.   cm. — (Enchantment of the world)
    Includes index.
    Summary: An introduction to the largest island in the world.
    ISBN 0-516-02710-7
    1. Greenland—Juvenile
literature. [1. Greenland.] I. Title. II. Series.
G743.L4 1989   88-37374
998'.2—dc19   CIP
                                                            AC

Picture Acknowledgments
© **Shostal Associates, Inc.:** 4, 6 (bottom), 13, 62, 77, 91, 111; © George Hunter: Cover, 52; © Ron Singer; 19
© **Superstock International, Inc.:** 5, 16
Valan Photos: © Fred Bruemmer: 6 (top), 20, 21, 46 (2 photos), 48, 68 (bottom right), 70, 72 (right), 79 (bottom left), 88, 89, 100 (right); © Stephen J. Krasemann: 64, 65 (left), 66 (left), 68 (top), 72 (left center); © Pam Hickman: 66 (right); © B. Lyon: 68 (bottom left): © Robert C. Simpson: 71 (center top); © Thomas Kitchin: 71 (center bottom); © W. Hoek: 72 (top left)
© **Emilie U. Lepthien:** 8, 12, 17, 22, 26 (bottom), 30, 32, 35, 38, 40, 50 (2 photos), 60 (left), 76 (3 photos), 79 (top & bottom right), 80, 81 (bottom left & right), 83 (right), 86 (2 photos), 93 (left), 95 (2 photos), 96, 99 (2 photos), 105 (right), 106, 107 (right), 108, 109, 110 (left), 114
Root Resources: © Bill Glass: 10, 26 (top), 107 (left); © Irene Hubbell: 23 (left), 78; © Kenneth W. Fink: 65 (right), 83 (left), 110 (right); © Alan G. Nelson: 71 (left); © Ben Goldstein: 71 (right); © Jane P. Downton: 23 (right), 81 (top), 93 (right), 94, 100 (left), 103, 105 (left)
© **Photri:** 14, 84 (left), 90, 92; © E. Culevant: 25
Historical Pictures Service, Chicago: 29, 37, 42, 55, 56 (right), 57 (2 photos), 58, 60 (right)
AP/Wide World Photos: 56 (left), 85 (right), 104
Culver Pictures: 59 (2 photos)
© **Jorgen B. Svensson:** 74, 82, 84 (right)
USA CCREL, Hanover, NH: 85 (left)
Len W. Meents: Maps on 9, 78, 80, 82
Courtesy Flag Research Center, Winchester, Massachusetts 01890: Flag on back cover
Cover: Ilulissat

TABLE OF CONTENTS

Left: An Inuit woman from Avanersuaq
Below: An aerial view of the southern tip of Greenland

Chapter 1

THE LARGEST ISLAND IN THE WORLD

Greenland is the largest island in the world. The Greenlandic or Inuit name for this island is *Kalaallit Nunaat*, which means "land of the people." Its area is 844,019 square miles (2,186,010 square kilometers).

GREENLAND'S INUIT PEOPLE

Approximately fifty-four thousand people live on Greenland. For over four thousand years, people have lived here. The original inhabitants crossed from Siberia and migrated east across North America.

ICE CAP, WEATHER, AND THE MIDNIGHT SUN

Greenland is a land of contrasts. The ice cap in the center covers more than 700,000 square miles (more than 1,800,000 square kilometers), and its maximum thickness is about 2 miles (3 kilometers), while the average thickness is about 1 mile (1.5 kilometers). It is the largest ice mass found outside Antarctica. The

A glacier near Narsaq reaches down to the sea.

ice moves down toward the coasts in great glaciers. When the glaciers reach the sea, huge chunks break off as icebergs. These icebergs generally float southward. It may take years for them to melt. They can be hazardous far down into the Atlantic Ocean.

Most of Greenland lies north of the Arctic Circle and warm weather is rare. During the winter north of the Arctic Circle there are weeks, even months, when the sun does not rise above the horizon. During this period of twilight and darkness, the temperature remains far below freezing for months.

North of the Arctic Circle in the summer, the sun stays above the horizon for weeks. The temperature along the coast then might average forty-six to fifty degrees Fahrenheit (eight to ten degrees Celsius). In the more protected fjords, the temperature will often be much higher.

CHALLENGES

Greenland presents a challenge to its people. They have proven they are capable of enduring long, cold winters. The Inuit have adapted to modern ways, but they also are anxious to maintain their culture that is part of the enchantment of Greenland.

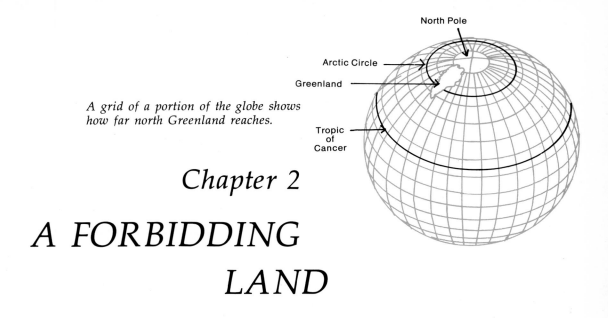

A grid of a portion of the globe shows
how far north Greenland reaches.

Chapter 2

A FORBIDDING
LAND

Greenland, the world's largest island, is located where the
North Atlantic Ocean meets the Arctic Ocean. The northern tip of
Greenland is 460 miles (740 kilometers) from the North Pole
across the Arctic Ocean. The southern tip is at about the same
latitude as Oslo, Norway. Greenland is about the same size as
Saudi Arabia or about three times the size of the state of Texas.
Almost 85 percent of the island is permanently covered with ice.
Only along the coasts are there some habitable ice-free areas,
particularly along the middle west coast and in the south.

HOW THE ISLAND WAS FORMED

Millions of years ago this enormous island and Canadian
islands to the west were part of the North American continent. It
is thought continental drift caused the land to separate.

Geologists working in the Nuuk (Godthåb in Danish) region

Climbers crossing a glacier

discovered rocks that were formed between 3,000 and 3,700 million years ago. Some rocks were volcanic. Some were sedimentary rocks, formed from clay and sandstone.

The earth's crust has been eroded by wind, ice, and air. In some regions near Nuuk, granite that lay fifteen miles (twenty-four kilometers) below the surface is exposed. The rock formations in Greenland are thought to be among the oldest in the world.

THE WORLD'S LARGEST ISLAND

The island is about 1,660 miles (2,670 kilometers) long from the extreme north to the southern tip. At its widest, Greenland is approximately 652 miles (1,050 kilometers) across. The coastline, with its many fjords, is 24,500 miles (39,427 kilometers).

Greenland is divided into three administrative divisions: North Greenland (Avannaa in Greenlandic), East Greenland (Tunu in Greenlandic), and West Greenland (Kitaa in Greenlandic). At the top, Cape Morris Jesup, bordering on the Arctic Ocean, is just 460 miles (740 kilometers) from the North Pole. Ellesmere Island, Canada, is a mere 17 miles (27 kilometers) northwest of Greenland.

On the east lies the Greenland Sea, an extension of the Arctic Ocean. Denmark Strait separates Greenland from Iceland, which is 250 miles (402 kilometers) to the east. Below Denmark Strait is the North Atlantic Ocean. At the southern edge of Greenland is Uummannarsuaq (Cape Farewell). On the west is the Labrador Sea. Nuuk is at about the same latitude as Fairbanks, Alaska. Above Nuuk, Davis Strait separates Greenland from Canada's Baffin Island. North of Davis Strait, Greenland borders on Baffin Bay.

THE GREAT ICE CAP

The interior of Greenland is a great plateau. The plateau's altitude measures from 4,000 to 9,000 feet (1,219 to 2,743 meters). Near the center of the island, the ice cap is 7,000 to 10,827 feet (2,133 to 3,300 meters) thick. The enormous weight of the ice has pressed the land itself below sea level.

The highest land is found along the coasts, especially the east. Mount Gunnbjørn's altitude is 12,247 feet (3,733 meters).

When flying over the ice cap, *nunataks* can be seen. They are mountains that look like islands in the glaciers. As the ice moves down from the cap, mountains divide the glaciers. In some places, moraines are formed from the stone and gravel the ice has scraped from the mountainsides. Finally, the glaciers reach the sea.

An icebound ship in the Ice Fjord at Ilulissat

ICEBERG ALLEYS

Cold ocean currents surround Greenland. The East Greenland Current carries icebergs south down the east coast, around Uummannarsuaq, and up the west coast almost as far north as Nuuk.

Ilulissat meaning icebergs (Jakobshavn in Danish), is situated on the west coast 175 miles (281 kilometers) north of the Arctic Circle. The city is located at the mouth of the Ice Fjord. Enormous icebergs calve (break off) from the Jakobshavn Glacier into the fjord as it moves down from the ice cap at 100 feet (30 meters) a day. Thousands of icebergs drift southward on the current. They present a great hazard to shipping. The International Ice Patrol conducted by the United States monitored with airplanes the movement of these icebergs for many years. Now the Danish and Greenland Iceberg Patrol covers the southern region. Since only one-tenth of an iceberg is above the water, those spotted from the air are much larger than seen.

A giant iceberg

Satellite radar planned for the near future will only detect icebergs 300 feet (91 meters) or larger in size. Satellite tracking of icebergs will not be available until the mid-1990s.

There are other glaciers on both coasts, but Jakobshavn Glacier is the most spectacular.

Each winter some snow is added to the ice cap, although the snowfall is light. The very cold temperatures reduce the amount of moisture the air can carry. Usually no more than 10 inches (22.5 centimeters) falls each year. It is like fine sand. Strong winds blow across the island, sweeping the snow clear in some areas even in the far north. The ice at the bottom of the ice cap fell as snow thousands of years ago. A slight warming trend in the past two decades has caused the glaciers to retreat.

There have been at least three major glacial epochs in the world. The last one in the Northern Hemisphere reached its maximum extent about fifteen to twenty thousand years ago. About eight thousand years ago the ice had retreated to the areas now covered.

Maximum temperature during the present warm period probably occurred between four and six thousand years ago. There were periods of cooling between 1000 and 400 B.C. Again the climate warmed from A.D. 800 to 1000, the time when the Vikings first settled on Greenland. But the climate cooled dramatically between A.D. 1300 and 1500 when the Viking settlers disappeared.

PERMAFROST

Perennially frozen ground is called permafrost. Most of Greenland is affected by permafrost. A ground layer on the surface thaws in summer and freezes again in winter. This layer may be 1.6 to 16 feet (45 to 487 centimeters) thick.

Buildings are built on permafrost, but also on the naked rock protruding everywhere in the towns. It is very costly to dynamite the ground to put the pipes down, so pipes are generally laid above ground. They must be heated electrically during cold weather. Some pipes are buried underground, but mostly in the bigger towns. Construction in Greenland, therefore, is very costly. This special construction is not necessary in southern Greenland.

LAND OF THE MIDNIGHT SUN

As the earth travels around the sun in a year, one pole is facing the sun for six months and away from the sun for the other six months. During the summer, when the North Pole is facing the sun, there is almost continuous sunlight, called the midnight sun,

A homeowner does some painting during the short summer season.

north of the Arctic Circle. The length of the period of the midnight sun depends upon how far north one goes. It occurs as far south as Sisimiut. However during the other six months of the year, called polar night, it is like twilight during the day. Real polar night, when there is no light at all, occurs in far northern Greenland.

When the sun rises above the horizon again in spring, the people in many places celebrate.

THE "WEATHER KITCHEN" OF EUROPE

Greenland has been called the weather kitchen of Europe. It is responsible for weather in countries to the east. Greenland's temperatures are low. The high mountains and especially the enormous ice cap affect the temperature. The permanent snow cover reflects heat from the sun. Even in the arctic summer, the

People enjoying the beach in Nuuk on a warm, sunny day

sun's rays reach the country at an angle. Maximum summer temperatures rarely get above freezing in much of the ice-free island.

Great winds sweep over the island. Even in summer temperatures sometimes drop sharply. Fog may suddenly encompass a region and then lift just as suddenly. The weather experienced one day in Greenland affects Europe a day or two later.

The western and southern parts of the ice sheet receive more snow than the north. The southwestern coastal region has a warmer and more moist climate. Except for floating icebergs, the ocean is ice free. In the summertime East Greenlandic pack ice drift around Uummannarsuaq and up along the west coast. It creates a lot of problems for ships and it even sometimes closes the harbors in Nanortalik, Qaqortoq (Julianehåb in Danish), and Narsaq. Sea ice does not form in the ocean. The harbor at Nuuk is open throughout the year. The wind, the cold, and the currents that travel down both east and west coasts combine to give Greenland the name "Europe's weather kitchen."

Chapter 3

THE INUIT

For more than 4,500 years, waves of immigrants have come to Greenland. Eskimo Stone Age culture began in Siberia perhaps five thousand years ago. People crossed the Bering Strait and moved east across the far north through what are now Alaska and Canada. The first Eskimo culture spread both to northeast and western Greenland.

THE SARQAQ CULTURE

Archaeologists call the first Stone Age people to reach West Greenland, in about 2500 B.C., the Sarqaq Culture. The name is due to the fact that the first remains were found near the village of Sarqaq in the Disko Bay region. Other remains have been found from Uummannaq to Nuuk. They were nomadic people who had hunted seals and caribou (called reindeer in Greenland) for hundreds of years as they moved east across North America to Greenland. They also hunted whales and birds.

Archaeologists have found various artifacts, soapstone lamps, stone points, and wooden and bone shafts used in hunting. The term "Eskimo" came from the Algonquin Indian name *Ush-ke-un-wau*, which meant "men who eat raw meat."

Hunters still use tents when they are away from home.

No one knows why these Stone Age nomadic Eskimos disappeared about three thousand years ago. Perhaps they left when the climate grew somewhat warmer and wetter. Perhaps they could not find the land and sea animals on which they depended.

THE DORSET CULTURES

Later another Stone Age Eskimo culture crossed from Canada to West Greenland. This was the Dorset Culture. The Dorset people arrived sometime around 600 B.C. and disappeared about eight hundred years later. The people were nomadic hunters. In summer they lived in skin tents. In winter some built snow

Sealskins are stretched on frames to dry.

houses. They cut snow blocks with their bone snow knives. They could build a snow house very quickly. Today we think of an igloo as a snow house, but in Eskimo "igloo" means any kind of house. Some dug pits and covered them with skins for protection from the winter cold. Seal oil was burned to provide some light and heat.

The Dorset Culture spread down the west coast. It is also known on the east coast. The Dorset I Culture probably disappeared when the climate grew colder about A.D. 250. The Dorset II Culture came to Greenland in the later part of the first millenium A.D. They probably stayed for about two hundred years. They are only known from the northwest Greenland area and very sporadically on the west coast.

THE INDEPENDENCE CULTURES

Meanwhile in northeast Greenland between 2500 and 2000 B.C., the Independence I Culture was established in what is now Peary

The remains of a house from the Thule Culture

Land. This culture inhabited the Independence Fjord and Peary Land area. Bone needles with round eyes, arrowheads, and lance heads have been found. The people hunted musk-oxen, seals, hares, foxes, and ptarmigans. These people were also nomadic. Between March and July, they lived in tent shelters. In winter they moved into shelters heated by burning driftwood and fatty bones. These people, too, disappeared.

About five hundred years later, from about 1400 to 600 B.C., the Independence II Culture lived in Peary Land. They used harpoons in hunting seals. Bone tools for scraping sealskins and needles for sewing skins have been found. The Independence II Eskimos lived in tents, too. Both the Independence I and II cultures probably used musk-ox skins for tents and bed covers.

THE THULE CULTURE

About A.D. 900 another group originated in Alaska. These were the Thule. They traveled east with their dog teams. By the year

A umiak stored upside down with a dog sled underneath it

1000 a few of these Eskimos reached the northwestern part of Greenland, formerly called the Thule District. By 1400 they had spread down the west coast. Many Thule sites have been found with remains of kayaks, oars, paddles, and larger sealskin boats called *umiaks* or "women's boats." Umiaks carried the family's belongings and family members. They also were used for whale hunting. Whales and seals were a chief source of food and fuel. They also hunted birds, reindeer, seals, and walruses.

Thule settlements were larger and the structures more solidly built than any of the other Eskimo cultures. They dug their houses into hillsides especially along the coast. Whalebones often served as rafters supporting turf roofs.

It is very likely that these people moved far enough south to encounter the Vikings who settled in southwestern Greenland. When Reverend Hans Egede from Norway settled on Hope

Island in the eighteenth century near present-day Nuuk, the Eskimos he met were the Thule Culture people. He called them "Greenlanders." Today's Inuit, or Greenlanders, are Thule descendants.

THE INUIT TODAY

It is possible that some Norsemen united with Inuit. (Inuit is not a specific group or culture. *Inuit* means "people" in Greenlandic.) Since the colonization, there have been many marriages between Inuit and Danes.

In 1970 there were approximately 140 towns and settlements in Greenland. Eighty-two of these have populations under one hundred. Many people were relocated, so they could have access to educational and medical facilities. Many Inuit settlements were included in this relocation. By 1985, the number of settlements were reduced to approximately 90.

The Inuit had lived for centuries hunting seals and other wildlife. Relocation caused many problems socially and in employment, housing, and services. Few jobs for which the Inuit were suited were available. The culture of the Inuit society was drastically changed.

The land and the sea have always been important to the Inuit. Whaling and seal hunting were traditional occupations for centuries. Now international organizations oppose whale and seal hunting. Fur trade has decreased. Inuit income has been reduced. The Inuit are concerned about environmental damage if offshore oil drilling begins in the future. The impact on their lives can be great if fishing and seal and subsistence whale hunting is disrupted.

Inuit children watch the same television programs as children in Europe and North America. Their parents fear that their culture will be lost. In the south and southwestern towns their culture has already been eroded by foreign standards.

POPULATION GROWTH

In 1901, there were less than 12,000 Greenlanders and fewer than 300 foreigners in Greenland. In 1985 the total population was 53,000. About 80 percent were born in Greenland. Most of the others were born in Denmark. They work in government or service positions. Many Danes stay in Greenland for only a few years.

THE GREENLANDIC OR INUIT LANGUAGE

Greenlandic has been designated by the Greenland government as the country's main language. It is unlike any other language.

An Inuit woman

Sometimes a single word expresses a sentence or several sentences. It is a difficult language for foreigners to learn.

Inuit in Alaska, Canada, and Greenland use the same language. However, there are differences in dialect and there is no common written language.

PRESERVING THE INUIT CULTURE

Through their language, music, and art, the Inuit hope to preserve their national culture. The original Greenlandic names are now replacing the Danish for towns and settlements. Home rule gives the Inuit the opportunity to make many decisions.

Every three years the Inuit Circumpolar Conference is held. Inuit from Alaska, Canada, and Greenland meet to discuss common problems. Siberian Inuit have been invited, too, and they will attend the meeting in 1989.

Permanent settlements are impossible on Greenland's ice cap or its mountains.

Chapter 4

WESTWARD TO GREENLAND

When Icelanders climbed a mountain on Snaefellsnes on a clear day, they saw what looked like snow-covered mountains to the west. Was it a mirage or really land?

OFF COURSE

About A.D. 900, Gunnbjørn Ulfsson's ship was blown west of Iceland by a storm. He found *skerries* (small islands) and beyond them what seemed to be land. The skerries, now named for Gunnbjørn, were rocky islets off the east coast of Greenland around the town of Ammassalik. For many years no one was interested in retracing Gunnbjørn's route.

THE FIRST SETTLEMENT

By 975 Iceland's western districts were completely settled. So in 978, Snaebjørn Galti sailed west with people who decided to find Gunnbjørn's islands.

The east coast of Greenland is sparsely inhabited even today. It is an inhospitable land. The colonists encountered a bitter winter.

Snowed in and lacking proper shelter and food, trouble broke out among the settlers. The survivors returned to Iceland as soon as the seas permitted in spring.

ERIC THE RED

Sagas have been written that tell how and why Eric the Red settled on Greenland.

Eric (Eirik) and his father, Thorvald, had to leave their home in Jaeren, Norway, because of some killings. By the time they arrived in Iceland, all of the best land had been taken. They settled at Dranger, where Thorvald died.

Eric, who must have been an impressive-looking redhaired man, was very enterprising. He married Thjodhild, whose father had extensive land. The couple moved south to Eiriksstadir near Vatnshorn, where their son Leif Ericsson may have been born.

Eric's temper again got him into trouble. After killing two men, he was forced to move. He went west to settle on Oxney Island in Breidafjord. He loaned a mainland farmer his bench boards, the two carved ends of the benches on which homeowners and their guests sat. When the farmer did not return the bench boards, a quarrel ensued. Several men were killed. Eric was banished from Iceland for outlawry for three years.

WHERE TO GO?

Eric could not return to Norway and he could not remain in Iceland. He had to seek a new place to live. The year was 982. He undoubtedly had heard of Gunnbjørn's discovery. He also must have heard about the ill-fated settlement of 978.

A painting shows Eric the Red's boat arriving in Greenland.

He readied a ship in Eiriksbay to sail west, promising to return at the end of his banishment. He hoped to find a good place to settle where he could be chieftain if others joined him later. He probably did not take his family on this sea voyage. It is thought a crew of twelve to twenty men accompanied him.

He sailed due west and found the land he sought. But the region looked uninhabitable. He sailed south along the coast looking for more suitable land. His first winter was spent on what he named "Eirik's Island" off the mouth of Eiriksfjord. In spring he sailed up the fjord and found a good place for his farm.

For the remaining two years he explored the southwestern section of the island looking for good pasturage. At the end of the three years he returned to Iceland.

He called the land he had explored "Greenland." He told his friends that people would be more interested in settling there if the place had an attractive name, and besides it was greener than Iceland.

Ruins of Eric the Red's farm near Narsarsuaq

COLONIZING GREENLAND

That summer Eric set sail for Greenland with twenty-five ships. The ships carried several hundreds of settlers and cattle, sheep, goats, and poultry. Food, tools, and some building materials were included also. Later, as in Iceland, supplies would have to come from Norway.

The colonists expected to build sod or turf houses like those in Iceland. Rocks and stones could be used also.

THE EASTERN AND WESTERN SETTLEMENTS

Some ships turned back; others were lost at sea. Fourteen ships with 450 colonists completed the journey. They settled in the southwestern part of Greenland. Theirs was the Eastern (or Østerbygden) Settlement. Eventually the settlement extended east to Cape Farewell. Eric and his family claimed the land he had found most suitable on his previous stay.

Two years later other settlers sailed farther north up the west coast. They established the Western (or Vesterbygden) Settlement. Their farms were near today's capital, Nuuk, in the huge fjord system east of the town.

EARLIER INHABITANTS

Near both settlements the colonists found remains of human habitation. Stone implements and fragments of skin boats were left behind by Eskimos who had spent perhaps a few months in each location. They had fished and hunted seals and reindeer. They settled in single farms spread all over the landscape where they could find grazing for their sheep, goats, and cattle. Remains of their farms can still be found.

FERTILE LAND

The climate was warmer than today. There was ample grass for the livestock. As in Iceland, each landholding was quite large. Travel between the farms and settlements was by boat or overland with horses.

Only hardy, hard-working colonists could settle so far from Norway and even Iceland. Ships with supplies could reach them only a few months each year. But for almost five hundred years, colonists remained on Greenland. Then they disappeared.

Remains of Thjodhild's chapel at Brattahlid

Chapter 5

THE NORSE SETTLEMENTS ON GREENLAND

CHRISTIANITY COMES TO GREENLAND

Iceland was still a pagan country when the first colonists came to Greenland. However Christianity came to Greenland, there is ample evidence that the settlers did abandon pagan ways. It is thought Leif Ericsson brought it from Norway around 1000.

Leif's mother, Thjodhild, was converted to Christianity and baptized. She had a small turf-and-wood chapel built near their farm, Brattahlid. Remains of the chapel and farm were recently uncovered by archaeologists. Eric's descendants continued to live at Brattahlid long after his death.

A Norwegian bishop named Arnald arrived in 1125. The cathedral of St. Nicholas, the patron saint of sailors, was built at Gardar. The cathedral was nearly one-hundred-feet (thirty-meters) long. In 1926, remains of this stone church, the bishop's house, stables, and the grave of Bishop Jan Smyrild, who became bishop in 1188 and died in 1209, were uncovered.

THE SETTLEMENTS GROW

Within 130 years after Eric the Red's first landing, the Norse population was between three and four thousand. The first settlers came from Iceland. Later, others who came were of Viking descent. Many children were born on Greenland.

ESTABLISHING LAW

Until 1260 Greenland was independent, but then the Greenlanders decided to join the kingdom of Norway. In exchange for this move, they were promised annual trading ships from Norway.

THE TWO SETTLEMENTS PROSPER

The settlements continued to prosper. By 1300 there were 190 farms in the Eastern Settlement. They were generally located in the fjords. The Eastern Settlement stretched from Narsaq to the southern tip of the island at Uummannarsuaq. There were twelve churches and two monasteries.

Eric's descendants and other farmers had good pasturage for their livestock. Some crops were raised.

The Western Settlement in the fjord region of Nuuk boasted ninety farms and four churches. There were fertile grazing areas in the deep fjord system in the Nuuk region. Sheep, cattle, goats, and horses had fine pasturage. Reindeer provided food, skins for clothing and shoes, and sinews for sewing. The antlers were made into handles for tools. Reindeer calfskins were exported as were walrus tusks, sealskin ropes, and *vadmel* (a cloth).

Sheep grazing in a lush summer field

ENCOUNTERS WITH THE ESKIMOS

The Eskimos were nomadic. They followed the seals and whales on which their lives depended. For many years there was little conflict between the Norse and the Eskimos. Later, when the Norsemen traveled north, conflicts did arise. The Norse called the Eskimos "Skraelings."

FARMERS, HUNTERS, AND FISHERMEN

The settlers lived by farming, hunting, and fishing. Ships arrived when the seas were relatively free of ice during the summer. Neither the Eastern nor Western settlement could be self-sufficient. The climate and short growing season limited the crops that could be raised.

The settlers had excellent woolen homespun fabric called vadmel, fish, sealskins, furs, tubs of butter, walrus tusks, and roping made from walrus hide to trade for lumber, iron tools, flour, and other supplies brought by Norwegian ships. For some years the Greenlanders had their own ships with which to carry on trade, principally with Norway.

EXPLORATIONS

Nuuk lies about 185 miles (300 kilometers) south of the Arctic Circle. For many years the coast north of Nuuk was not explored.

The Vikings were excellent sailors. They had sailed to many countries in Europe. In Iceland's *Book of Settlements* it was recorded: "It is seven days' sail from Stad in Norway to Horn in the east of Iceland. From Snaefellsnes [the west coast of Iceland] it is four days' sail to Cape Farewell in Greenland."

EXPLORATION CONTINUES

The explorations of Leif and his brothers who sailed west to North America were recorded in sagas. There were others who explored farther north on Greenland. Eric himself had spent many months sailing down the east coast from present-day Ammassalik and into the fjords.

In 1266, Halldor, a Greenlandic priest, wrote to a friend in Norway that some men had traveled farther north up the west coast than had any Europeans. These explorers paused at 75 degrees, 46 minutes north and then continued on farther north.

The Norsemen wrote in the runic alphabet, an arrangement of straight lines. It was used in many European countries from A.D. 200 until 1200, when Latin letters were adopted. Many runic carvings on wood and stone have been found in Norse settlements in Greenland where these symbols were still used as long as the settlements existed.

In many places men left cairns, or piles of rocks, to mark their route or to leave supplies. Sometimes they left messages on a cairn. A runic inscription left by three men on a cairn in the

Runic inscriptions were left by early explorers.

fourteenth century was found far north at latitude 72 degrees, 55 minutes north. It is incomplete but it reads: "Erling Sighvatsson and Bjarni Thordarsson and Eindridi Jonsson on the Saturday before the minor Rogation Day [April 25] built these cairns and cleared . . ." (Rogation Days are the three days before Ascension Day, a Christian holy day.)

TIES WITH ICELAND

Greenland's civilization was an extension of Iceland's. The two countries were linked by a common language and culture. Their houses, farms, and way of life were much alike. Communication with family and friends in Norway and Iceland was maintained by ship.

A sod and stone house from an early settlement is preserved as a reminder of Greenland's past.

A GREENLAND HOUSE

The houses were built of stone and sod. In the older houses there was one long room. The floor was of stone. Later houses were divided into small rooms, which were easier to heat.

Stone troughs or gutters brought water into the rear of the house, where the cooking was done. The source could be cut off by blocking the trough or gutter with stones.

The cold winter required housing for the animals also. A barn with stalls for forty cows was found at Eric's Brattahlid.

ICELANDIC SAGAS

Some Icelanders wrote about their life on Greenland. The *Sworn-Brothers Saga* described the hardships an Icelandic poet encountered on Greenland. *Floamanna Saga* tells the story of Thorgils, who sailed for Greenland intending to settle there. He found life very difficult in his new home. He returned to his farm in Iceland, bitter about his experiences. Not everyone was happy with life in the settlements.

THE NORSE SETTLEMENTS DISAPPEAR

For about five hundred years Norse settlers remained on Greenland. For several reasons it appears the settlements were doomed. The climate gradually worsened. It was the kind of mini-Ice Age that was felt on Iceland, also. No longer was the grass lush and green; fodder for the animals was scarce. Ships failed to come from Norway with much needed supplies. The Norsemen on Greenland lacked materials to maintain their own ships. In addition, Norway forbade trade on any but Norwegian ships

Unlike the Eskimos who were nomadic, hunting for seals, whales, and walruses, the settlers had built permanent homes. Without supplies from the mother country, they could not survive.

There also were bloody encounters between the Eskimos and the settlers. The Eskimos had moved farther south as encroaching ice drove the seals farther down the west coast.

There is no definite record of who were the last Norse survivors or how the settlements perished. It is thought the Western Settlement colonists perished first. Ivar Bardarson visited Greenland and stayed for over twenty years. After he left he wrote, "The horses, sheep, goats, and cattle are wild. Now the Skraelings [Eskimos] have the entire West Settlement." Perhaps

A bronze sculpture, with symbolic figures,
shows the plans of Eric's farm at Brattahlid.

some of the people in the Western Settlement packed their
belongings and moved to the Eastern Settlement.

The Eastern Settlement survived into the fifteenth century. One
report tells of a Skraeling assault in 1379 in which eighteen
Norsemen in a hunting party were killed.

But eventually the Norse settlements were empty. What
happened to the Norse farmers is still a mystery. No one knows.
The last information about the Norse settlement is an Icelandic
record mentioning a marriage on April 16, 1408 in the Hvalsø
Church in the Eastern Settlement. About four hundred Norse
ruins have been discovered. Of these, three hundred are of farms
of different sizes and periods.

When the Norse were gone, the Eskimos still remained. They
had lived on the island intermittently for extended periods for
four thousand years. Their nomadic life enabled them to survive.
Their next encounter with Western civilization would come
through contact with whalers, traders, explorers, and
missionaries.

Chapter 6

NORSEMEN SAIL TO NORTH AMERICA

The hardy men and women who first settled Greenland found good pasturage and a climate not too unlike Iceland. They farmed, but much of their food came from the sea where they fished and went sealing and whaling.

And true to their Viking heritage, they went exploring. The Vikings were incredible sailors. Their sturdy ship, called a *knorr*, was built of oak. A large square sail could be adjusted to make the best use of the wind. Sixteen pairs of oars could move the knorr when the wind was calm.

The knorr was not much more than 50 feet (15 meters) long with a 15-foot (4.5-meter) beam. Colonists, livestock, and supplies were crammed into these small ships. Knerrir (plural for knorr) carried cargo between Norway and Iceland and later to Greenland. It was probably a ship like this that Leif used on his voyage of discovery.

Herjolf Bardarson accompanied Eric the Red to Greenland. Herjolf's son, Bjarni, was a prosperous merchant on the Iceland-Norway trade route. He alternated his winters between the two countries. When he returned to Iceland in A.D. 986, he found his father had emigrated to Greenland.

The knorr used by Viking sailors had sails and sixteen pairs of oars that were used when the wind was calm.

BJARNI SIGHTS NORTH AMERICA

Bjarni decided not to unload his cargo. Instead, he and his crew set sail for Greenland. But they were blown off course. Eventually they sailed close to three different land masses. Two were forested. The men wanted to take on fresh water and wood, but Bjarni refused. Instead, he sailed back, finally reaching his father's farm, Herjolfsnes, in the south of Greenland. Had Bjarni gone ashore he would have been the first European to step foot on North America. Instead, that honor went to Leif, Eric's son.

LEIF SAILS WEST

Leif was excited about Bjarni's discovery. He urged his father to join him in searching for this new land to the west. But Eric said he was too old for such travels. Leif bought Bjarni's ship, hired a crew of thirty-five, and set sail on a voyage of discovery about A.D. 1000.

His first landfall was probably on Baffin Island. He called the place Helluland, Slab-land; there was no grass on the barren shore. For many years ships sailing to Vinland used the place as a landfall.

Leif went ashore at his second landfall. He named the place Mark-land, Forest Land. It was probably Labrador.

THE THIRD LANDFALL

Again, Leif took to the sea. In a few days he sighted land and went ashore. This was his most important landing. The grass was thick and there were trees. Salmon abounded in the rivers and lake. Leif and his crew decided to spend the winter. They built stone and turf shelters roofed with awnings, which were called "booths," or *Leifsbudir.*

Tyrkir, a German who had lived with Erik the Red's family, accompanied Leif on the journey. Leif called him his foster father. Tyrkir left camp and explored inland alone. Leif worried about his friend's safety. But tales say when Tyrkir returned to camp he was excited. He reported finding grapes like those he had seen growing in Germany. Leif and his crew were very happy. In spring they returned to Greenland with timber.

Leif called the place Vinland. *Vin* in Old Norse means a field of green grass or meadow. Although he did not return, he encouraged others to sail there. Later when his brothers asked to buy Leifsbudir, he would not sell them. Instead he leased his shelters to the travelers.

VINLAND THE GOOD

No one is positive where Vinland was in North America. Archaeologists have uncovered the remains of Norse structures at

L'Anse aux Meadows, Newfoundland. It may have been a base camp for other Norse explorers. Was it Vinland? Probably it was. Vikings roamed as far south from the Gulf of St. Lawrence to Massachusetts or Rhode Island.

There were large salmon in the rivers and lake. The grass barely withered in winter, since there was no frost. Night and day were of almost equal length. It was a good land.

THORVALD AND THORSTEIN

Leif's brother Thorvald used the ship to return to Vinland in 1004. He and his crew wintered in Leif's "booths." The following year when exploring down the coast, they were attacked by Skraelings. Thorvald was mortally wounded. The crew spent another winter at Leif's booths and then returned to Greenland.

Leif's other brother, Thorstein, asked to use Leif's ship to sail to Vinland. He wanted to bring his brother's body back to Greenland for Christian burial.

However, bad weather prevented him and his crew from reaching Vinland. Instead they turned back and took refuge in the Western Settlement on Greenland. That winter disease struck the settlement and Thorstein and many of his crew died. Thorstein's wife Gudrid, who was on the ill-fated trip, survived. Later she returned to Brattahlid.

THORFINN KARLSEFNI ARRIVES IN GREENLAND

That summer Thorfinn Karlsefni, an Icelandic merchant, arrived at Brattahlid. He fell in love with Gudrid and at Christmas the two were married. They decided to sail west to Leif's Vinland, too.

In 1011, with sixty men, five women, livestock, and supplies, Thorfinn and Gudrid sailed to Vinland to establish a permanent settlement. They found Leifsbudir easily. The men carried their hammocks ashore. Their cattle found good forage. Fish and wild game were abundant. The first winter passed without difficulty.

The next summer Skraelings appeared. They carried pelts and furs, which the Norse exchanged for milk. The Skraelings left, satisfied with their trade.

During the three years they spent in Vinland, Snorri, Thorfinn and Gudrid's son, was born. He was the first "white" child born in North America.

The next summer when the Skraelings returned to trade furs and pelts, they tried to steal weapons. A battle ensued. The Skraelings fled, but Thorfinn decided the colonists should leave the following year. They returned to Greenland with timber, pelts, dried grapes, and other produce.

Thorfinn Karlsefni and his party had established the first permanent "European" settlement in North America.

FREYDIS GOES TO VINLAND

Two brothers moved to Greenland and settled at Gardar. Freydis, Eric's daughter, went to see them. She convinced them to hire a crew, equip a ship, and accompany her ship to Vinland. She offered to share equally any profits from the trip.

Freydis was a scheming woman. She wanted all of the profits. The ships landed at Leif's booths. In a short time, Freydis found a way to have her crew kill everyone from the other ship. The following spring she set sail for Greenland. The second ship was loaded with produce. The profits were all hers.

Above: Great skill is needed to propel sealskin kayaks.
These hunters have tied their kayaks together to tow a narwhal to shore.
Below: Greenlanders hunt, using guns and harpoons, only
for as much as they need to support life.

Chapter 7

GREENLAND REDISCOVERED

For generations the Eskimos had lived primarily from the sea. They knew where hunting for whales and seals was best. The colonists had found remains of Eskimo skin boats and tools as far south as the Eastern Settlement.

THE ESKIMO SEALERS

The Eskimos hunted reindeer, foxes, polar bears, seals, and whales. They fished and used darts to kill birds. To hunt seals, Eskimos paddled their kayaks quietly up to animals languishing on ice floes or attacked them in the water when they came up for air.

Eskimo spears or harpoons were generally driftwood tipped with bone or iron. They may even have found iron objects in abandoned Norse buildings or in shipwrecks. The Thule Culture people also used iron from the iron meteorites found in the southern part of the Avanersuaq district close to the settlement Savissivik. Later the Eskimos traded pelts for metal tools and spearheads.

Eskimo men were experts in handling their sealskin kayaks. Their kayaks were built strong enough to carry a seal in back of

A woman chews on a piece of sealskin to make it more pliable for use as a boot sole.

the cockpit. The sealers also had other ways to float or bring their catch to shore.

Generally women did the flensing—skinning and preparing the seals (and whales) for food and other uses. Seals filled almost all the Eskimos' needs.

WHALING

Whales became an important source of income for many countries in the seventeenth and eighteenth centuries. The Greenland Sea on the east and Melville Bay, Davis Strait, and Disko Bay off the west coast became important whaling areas for British, Dutch, German, Danish, Norwegian, and American whalers. Huge right whales were caught in the cold waters off Greenland in the 1700s. Often ships were lost in the crush of ice.

When a whale had been killed, it was brought alongside the ship. There the men began to cut the blubber from the flesh. In some regions, the blubber was packed in casks. Or at a shore station, the blubber was chopped into small pieces and boiled. The oil was extracted and put in casks, which were floated back to the whaler.

Whale oil was burned in lamps until kerosene became popular. The oil also was used as a lubricant. Whalebone or baleen, the long fibrous strands in the whale's mouth, was carefully cleaned and packed into bundles of sixty. Baleen was used in umbrellas, ladies' dresses, and undergarments. Whale meat was sold in markets.

To be successful, a whaler had to catch at least three whales before returning to home port. Often several ships worked together.

THE DUTCH WHALERS

Of all the ships in the seas around Greenland, the Dutch were the most aggressive. They sent dozens of ships into arctic waters covering the area from Spitsbergen, Norway, to Greenland. The Dutch set up trading posts on Greenland's west coast. They obtained pelts and blubber from the Eskimos who gladly traded for European items.

HANS EGEDE, MISSIONARY AND TRADER

Hans Egede was a Norwegian Lutheran minister. He wondered what had happened to the Norsemen on Greenland. He wanted to make certain that any Norse descendants who remained were still Christians. In 1721 he convinced the Danish king to combine missionary work and trade with the Eskimos.

Above: The house built by Reverend Hans Egede is now the residence of Greenland's premier.
Left: A statue of Egede in Nuuk

Reverend Egede and his family sailed to Greenland on the *Hope*. They landed on a small island off the west coast of Greenland and called it Haabets O (Hope Island). The people aboard the *Hope* built a turf house. Each morning Eskimos, whom Egede called Greenlanders, came to help. Poul and Niels Egede, the two sons, made friends with Greenland boys. Poul began to make a dictionary of their words.

TRADING WITH THE GREENLANDERS

Other Danish ships came to Greenland to trade with the Eskimos. They returned to Denmark with fox and seal skins, whalebone, and blubber. But the Danes were not as successful as the Dutch in whaling and trading.

BUILDING ON THE MAINLAND

Later Egede traveled around to see where Norsemen had lived over two hundred years earlier. There were no Norsemen alive. So he decided to become a missionary to the Greenlanders. The Egedes spent seven years on the island. Then Egede found a suitable site on the mainland for a settlement.

In 1728 he moved to what became the first modern European settlement on Greenland. He called it Godthåb, Good Hope, now the capital of the country. Its Greenlandic name is Nuuk, which means "promontory."

CHRISTIANITY COMES TO GREENLAND NATIVES

Many of the Greenlanders came to Pastor Egede to become Christians. Poul translated the Lord's Prayer into Greenlandic. Instead of "Give us this day our daily bread," he had to write "Give us this day our daily meat." Poul also translated the New Testament into Greenlandic.

Poul served as a Lutheran minister in Greenland. Hans returned to Denmark after seventeen years. He is honored today as the "Apostle of Greenland."

THE GERMAN MORAVIANS

In 1733 Moravian missionaries came to Nuuk from Germany. The Greenlanders enjoyed singing. They particularly liked the accompaniment of the small organ the Moravians brought. The Lutheran and Moravian missionaries worked independently. The Moravian mission, built in 1747, now houses Ilisimatusarfik, Greenland University.

Fishing boats in the inner harbor at Ilulissat

GREENLAND REMAINS DANISH

Niels Egede worked as a trader for Jacob Severin, who had the Norwegian-Danish trading monopoly for Greenland. Dutch whalers and traders came often to Greenland in these years (1730s-1740s). Severin's ships once entered into a gunfight with them to keep them from trading with the Inuit. That happened in Makelijk Oud in 1739. Later on, in 1741, a trading post and missionary station was established there by Jacob Severin and he called it Jacobshavn (present-day Ilulissat) after himself. Through the efforts of Hans Egede and his family and Jacob Severin the merchant, Greenland remained under the Danish-Norwegian government.

In 1776, the government set up the Royal Greenland Trading Company. For the next 170 years, no other country could trade with Greenland. In 1814, Norway became a separate country. No mention was made of Greenland. So it remained a Danish colony.

Chapter 8

GREENLAND EXPLORED

ATUAGAGDLIUTIT

In 1855 the scientist, Dr. Hinrich Rink, was appointed superintendent of the southern part of Greenland at Qaqortoq. He settled in Nuuk. He was a very progressive man who wanted the Inuit to take more part in the administration of their country. In 1861 Rink started a newspaper, *Atuagagdliutit* (*Reading*), which is still published. Lars Møller, a fifteen-year-old Inuit, helped him. Lars Møller later was sole editor and printer of the newspaper from 1873 to 1922. He was one of the most outstanding Inuit of that time. It was he who introduced the knowledge of the Inuit in Greenland to other parts of the world. He had Greenlanders write about their lives. He also published news from other parts of the world. The Greenlanders—Inuit—were learning about the outside world.

Rink collected Inuit stories and legends and a very important collection of watercolor drawings by the famous Aron from Kangeq.

The important advances in Greenlandic education in the Inuit (Greenlandic) language are the result of their efforts as well as those of Hans Egede.

SCIENTIFIC STUDIES

Scientists were interested in studying Greenland's ice cap. Dr. Hinrich Rink arrived in Greenland in 1848 expecting to spend a year in geological and geographical research. Instead, he remained for twenty years and recorded not only the natural resources but the culture and conditions of the Eskimos.

Dr. Rink's studies of the ice sheet spurred further research. That interest continues in expeditions conducted by American and Danish scientists. They measure the depth of the ice, its age, and rate at which glaciers move. Ice cores from central Greenland reach back hundreds of thousands of years. They demonstrate climatic changes and pollution.

Scientists use large drills that are heated. They melt their way down as they core into the ice. Ice cores about 6 inches (15 centimeters) in diameter and 5 feet (1.5 meters) long are carefully brought up, one after another. Some of the ice cores have come from hundreds of feet below the surface. Ice cores brought up at Camp Century were examined.

Now these studies are conducted on the ice cap in central and southern Greenland. The ice was formed hundreds of thousands of years ago. Scientists study these cores to note climatic changes and pollution that occurred through the centuries. In the future scientists hope to study ice cores from a million years ago. Camp Century can no longer be used. Its walls have collapsed and snows have covered the site.

Martin Frobisher

THE NORTHWEST PASSAGE

For centuries sailors sought a northeast passage from Siberia to the Atlantic Ocean. Others searched for a northwest passage from the other way. The British and Spanish were concerned about Russian settlements in Alaska and down the North American coast as far as San Francisco. A short route between the Atlantic and Pacific oceans would protect their interests and increase trade with the Orient.

Greenland played an important role in the search. Expeditions set out from northern Greenland and many lives and ships were lost.

In the sixteenth century, navigators sought a water passage to China across the north from the Atlantic to the Pacific Ocean. Martin Frobisher, a British sea captain, rounded Cape Farewell in 1576 and sailed west to what is now Frobisher Bay in southeast Baffin Island. In 1578, Frobisher spent some time with Eskimos on Greenland's west coast.

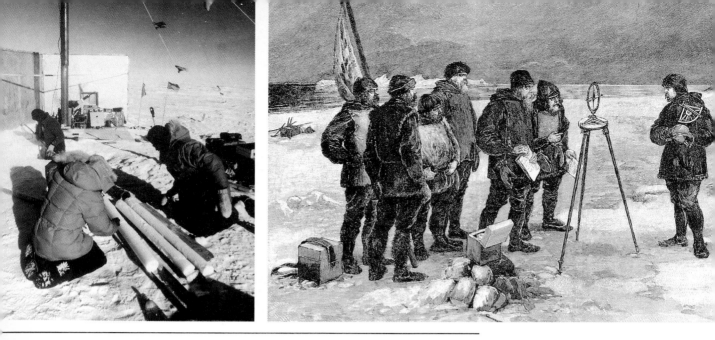

Left: Scientists studying ice cores, which give them information about climate, geological history, and man-made pollution.
Right: A painting showing the discovery of the magnetic pole

In 1587, John Davis landed near Nuuk. Davis Strait is named for him. He called the east coast a land of desolation.

There were other explorers who visited Greenland. In 1616 William Baffin, an English navigator, sailed up the west coast to Upernavik and Avanersuaq.

Captain John Ross visited the Eskimos in the far north in 1818. He called them Arctic Highlanders. John Ross, a British sea captain, led several expeditions to find the Northwest Passage. He wasn't successful and was marooned in far northern Greenland for four years. A group of Polar Eskimos, who thought they were the only people in the world, helped his party survive.

John Clark Ross, his nephew, accompanied him on one expedition and discovered the North Magnetic Pole. The North Magnetic Pole moves about 69 miles (111 kilometers) in ten years. The movement of the magnetic pole results from the motion of the hot liquid metal, mostly iron and nickel, in the earth's core. Both the North and South Magnetic Poles shift.

John Franklin (left) died trying to find the Northwest Passage and a boat from his expedition (right) was found later.

In 1822, Captain William Scoresby explored Greenland's northeast coast. Captain Scoresby drew the first accurate map of the 800 miles (1,287 kilometers) of coast north of the Arctic Circle. He landed in many places and made notes of the flora and fauna. He also found abandoned Eskimo camps. Scoresbysund on the east coast, now called Illoqqortoormiut, was originally named for him. There were many other British, Danish, and American sea captains who explored the coast.

Sir John Franklin's ill-fated expedition, from 1845-48, came within 3 miles (4.8 kilometers) of the Northwest Passage. Robert McClure is credited with first sighting it. Roald Amundsen was the first to traverse it in 1904-06. The first commercial ship to negotiate the Northwest Passage was the S. S. *Manhattan*, an icebreaking tanker, in 1969.

EXPLORATIONS CONTINUE

Not only the Northwest Passage interested explorers. The ice cap invited explorations. Beginning in the eighteenth century, men tried to penetrate the interior. They tried crossing from west to east. None were successful.

Fridtjof Nansen (left) and members of his exploring party

NANSEN AND PEARY

There were many explorers who sought to penetrate Greenland's ice cap. Those who set out from the west coast found the crossing impossible. In 1888, Fridtjof Nansen, a Norwegian, and five companions made the first successful crossing from the east to west coast. They were beset with snowstorms and intense cold. They had reached an altitude of 8,250 feet (2,515 meters). They crossed deep crevasses. Finally, they saw bare ground ahead. The last ship had left port, so they wintered in Nuuk.

American Lieutenant Robert E. Peary led several expeditions to Greenland. In 1891-92, he led the North Greenland Expedition to obtain a collection of Eskimo artifacts for the World's Columbian Exposition in Chicago in 1893.

The party wintered in a permanent house built of stone and wood. Eskimos arrived at the base and were carefully studied. Peary took many photographs of the Eskimos. He and Dr. Frederick Cook exchanged tools and lumber for ethnographic objects such as harpoons, spears, skin pots, and clothing from the Eskimos. Peary explored farther north to Independence Fjord.

The Roosevelt *(left), a ship designed and used by Robert E. Peary (right) in his explorations.*

When Peary returned to the United States, much of his collection was displayed at the Columbian Exposition. Later it was turned over to the Field Museum in Chicago.

Promoted to commander, Peary returned several more times to Greenland. He determined that Greenland was an island. In his journey to the far north he discovered a barren area without ice and snow. It is now called Peary Land in his honor.

Commander Peary claimed he reached the North Pole with his assistant Matthew Henson and four Eskimos on April 6, 1909. Dr. Frederick Cook claimed he had reached the North Pole a year earlier. However, Peary's claim was accepted and Cook's was considered false. Peary was promoted to rear admiral for his accomplishment.

KNUD RASMUSSEN

Knud Rasmussen, Greenland's native son, was its most famous explorer. In 1910 he opened a trading post he named Thule. He felt these isolated Eskimos needed a place to trade hides, tusks,

The home (left) of Knud Rasmussen (right) is now a museum in Ilulissat.

and other items for supplies such as rifles and ammunition, cooking utensils, and metal tools that would make life easier.

Peter Freuchen assisted Rasmussen in this endeavor. Rasmussen and Freuchen crossed the ice cap in 1912. Rasmussen led five more expeditions in northern Greenland. He mapped much of that uncharted region between 1913 and 1931. He was awarded honorary doctorate degrees for his scientific studies of the Eskimos, the inland ice, and the coasts. His sixth expedition was conducted in 1931. The house in Ilulissat where he was born in 1879 is now a museum. He died in 1933. A region in the far northwest is named for him. He was the first man to consider Thule a future site for an air base.

OTHER EXPLORERS

Fascinated by the ice cap, explorers from many countries attempted and completed crossings. Denmark established the Danish Expeditions Fund to encourage Greenland scientific explorations. On some of these programs, ships and Catalina flying boats as well as dogs and sleds were used to reach their destinations.

On the shore of Jørgen Brønlunds Fjord in Peary Land, the Danes established a base 540 miles (869 kilometers) from the North Pole in 1948 under the leadership of Count Eigil Knuth. Windmills were erected to generate electricity for radio transmission and lighting. Weather reports were transmitted to Copenhagen every six hours. They even picked up a greeting from the Norwegian-British-Swedish expedition at the South Pole as well as contacting amateur radio operators throughout the world.

The geologists studied the rock strata. Other scientists identified dozens of plant specimens, twenty-one bird species, insects, various sea animals, and land animals.

The sites of Eskimo ruins were found just 470 miles (756 kilometers) from the North Pole. A 35-foot (10-meter) umiak and tools were discovered 150 miles (241 kilometers) from the fjord base at the coast. A radiocarbon dating on the boat showed that it was five hundred years old. The specimens and artifacts were sent to the National Museum in Copenhagen, Denmark.

IS GREENLAND MORE THAN ONE ISLAND?

The British, French, and Americans have conducted further research. Echo soundings on the ice cap seem to indicate that Greenland is separated into three parts covered by one enormous ice sheet.

Greenland continues to draw scientists from many universities to study the world's second largest ice sheet and its unique Eskimo—Inuit—population.

A view of the coast between Nuuk and Qorqut

Chapter 9

LAND, AIR, AND SEA

Six-sevenths of Greenland is permanently covered by the ice cap. The ice-free areas hug the coast. It is in these areas, principally along the southern and midsections of West Greenland, that the towns and settlements are found.

Even the ice-free areas are wild and mountainous. The ice-free area at Kangerlussuaq (Søndre Strømfjord in Danish) on the west coast reaches a width of 120 miles (193 kilometers). It is one of the larger ice-free areas in the country.

NATIONAL PARK AND RESEARCH AREA

In 1974 Greenland's National Park was established in the far north and northeast. It is the world's largest national park. It covers over one-fourth of the island. The boundaries were suggested by the Commission for Scientific Research in Greenland. Except for the less than thirty-five persons at the permanent military and weather stations, the entire area is uninhabited.

There are large ice-free coastal areas in the region closest to Ellesmere Island, across Greenland's Peary Land, and down the

A reindeer with magnificent antlers

northeast coast to Illoqqortoormiut, 71 north latitude. The park is a large scientific research area, but it is open to the public also.

A WIDE RANGE OF CLIMATE

The entire island has an arctic climate. The northern tip of Greenland is only 460 miles (740 kilometers) from the North Pole. The Polar Sea is ice covered. The cold East Greenland Current makes the east coast almost uninhabitable. From here giant icebergs move south and eventually sweep some distance up the west coast.

Uummannarsuaq at the southern tip is 550 miles (885 kilometers) south of the Arctic Circle. Here the Gulf Stream creates a warmer climate.

In the southwestern region, farmers today raise sheep, horses, and some reindeer. Some winters, frost and snows cause great livestock losses. But during the summer pasturage is good.

Dwarf arctic birch (left) and scrub willow (right)

A TIME LONG PAST

Millions of years ago the island had a warm temperate climate like southern Europe. Scientists have discovered fossils of leaves from such trees as the fig and magnolia. But all of this changed through time. After the Ice Age, when the ice melted in other parts of the Northern Hemisphere, Greenland's ice cap remained.

GREENLAND'S TREES

Now there are few trees on the entire island. Most deciduous trees, those that lose their leaves, grow in sheltered fjords in the south of Greenland. Alder, willow, and dwarf arctic birch form thickets or small woods. There are some other shrubs in this region.

In the low or subarctic zone below the Arctic Circle, flowers abound in summer. Scrub willow and birch may grow as tall as a person.

Crowberries (left) and arctic cotton grass (right)

In the high Arctic, north of the Arctic Circle, trees seldom grow taller than a foot (thirty centimeters) or more. They may be hundreds of years old, since their annual gowth is very small. Only the hardiest plants can survive the short growing season, the sometimes thin snow cover, and the strong winter gales.

The line between the high and low or subarctic regions is not sharply defined. Weather conditions and temperature are affected by the location.

OTHER PLANTS WITH SAP

Over two hundred years ago Poul Egede made the first collection of vascular plants, plants with sap. They include members of the rose, mustard, saxifrage, heath, daisy, grass, crowfoot, and sedge families. One of the important shrubs was the crowberry. The berries were a part of the Eskimo diet. The Egede family on Hope Island enjoyed them, too.

There are about five hundred different vascular plants in Greenland. Of these more than forty are high Arctic. Mountain avens, capitate lousewort, white arctic bell-heather, and the high arctic spider plant flower in far north. Alpine cress can be found all over the island.

The pale yellow arctic poppy and white cotton grass, found also in Iceland, grow throughout the country. Ferns grow under the trees in the south of Greenland.

GREENLAND'S OTHER PLANTS

The ground is not altogether barren, even where there are no grasses or sedges. There are about 3,500 species of algae, fungi, lichens, and mosses.

LAND MAMMALS

Very few animals have adapted to the harsh arctic environment. There are four herbivores, or vegetarians, and four carnivores, or meat eaters. None of Greenland's mammals hibernate. Even in the winter darkness they must forage for food.

The herbivores include the musk-ox, wild reindeer, hare, and lemming. Vegetation is very sparse in most ice-free areas. So the grazing animals are widely scattered. Carnivores, therefore, often have a difficult time catching their food.

HERBIVORES

The musk-oxen are some of Greenland's oldest inhabitants. Recently they were threatened with extinction. Now they are

*Some of the animals found in Greenland include the musk ox (above),
the lemming (below left), and the arctic hare (below right).*

protected. Their long under hair is the world's lightest and warmest wool.

When reindeer, sometimes called caribou, crossed from Canada is not known, but they were in Greenland before 3000 B.C.

Arctic hare are white throughout the year. Their great speed helps them escape their enemies. Greenlanders like their soft, warm fur and use it for clothing. The fur is often worn inside against the wearer's skin. The Greenlanders also enjoy the meat.

The lemming is the smallest and most numerous animal in the Arctic. In a harsh year, when the lemming population is reduced, the arctic fox and the ermine go hungry.

CARNIVORES

The ermine and white arctic fox feed primarily on lemmings. The blue arctic fox lives near the shore where it scavenges on crabs, crayfish, and snails. In spring it finds seal dens on sea ice to feed on seal pups. Often blue foxes venture out on pack ice, following the polar bear. Greenlanders trap foxes for their fur.

Pack ice is a floating mass of sea ice formed in the polar seas. Sheets of ice cover the ocean surface. Drifting pack ice from the Arctic basin travels down the east coast of Greenland. By midsummer most of it has left Greenland waters.

The arctic wolf was not seen for many years. But since 1984 arctic wolves have been sighted. They also feed on lemmings, arctic foxes, hares, and musk-ox calves.

Polar bears can charge a resting seal at twenty-five miles (forty kilometers) an hour. Seals are their favorite diet. They also prey on other animals and birds' eggs. Layers of blubber keep polar bears warm in the water. On land, they are protected by an

Arctic foxes trailing a polar bear

underlayer of dense wool and long guard hairs. The Inuit name for polar bear is *nanoq*. Many large adult males are much taller than a man when they are standing on their hind legs.

BIRDS

More than fifty species of birds breed on Greenland. Puffins, snow buntings, grouse, white-tailed eagles, and snowy owls are easily found.

The arctic tern breeds on Greenland in summer. Then it flies over 9,000 miles (14,484 kilometers) to winter in Antarctica's summer.

Eider ducks' soft feathers and their eggs have made them favorite birds with the Inuit for many years.

Some of Greenland's birds, clockwise from top center, are: the eider duck, the puffin, the snowy owl, and the white gyrfalcon.

Kittiwakes, fulmers, gulls, and ravens are found in many regions. The white gyrfalcon and the white-tailed eagle now are protected from hunting. The ptarmigan provided a pleasant change in the Eskimos' diet.

ANIMALS OF THE SEA

The ringed seal, Greenland seal, and other types have supplied the Inuit with almost all of their needs for centuries. About five thousand people depend on sealing and hunting for their livelihood today. Between eighty and ninety thousand adult seals are caught annually. The Inuit never kill baby seals.

Right whales, white whales, narwhals, and walruses are hunted. Twenty-five hundred minke whales, narwhals, porpoises, white

Top Left: White whales
Left: Walruses basking in the sun.
Above: A Greenland seal pops up
through a hole in the ice.

whales, walruses, and humpback whales were caught in 1985. The most common whales to be hunted are the white whales, the narwhals, and the porpoises.

The whale and seal meat are very important in the Inuit diet. Only skins and tusks are exported. Until recent times, the Inuit hunted with harpoons often tipped with walrus ivory or the narwhal tusk. Today the hunters hunt both with traditional tools, such as the harpoons, and with modern harpoons and guns. The hunters are being taught to use modern whale-hunting techniques with the harpoons to prevent any loss of animals. Traditionally, Greenlanders have hunted only for as much as they need to support life. Hunting is not a sport, but is done for subsistence and is a vital part of the culture and daily life.

FISH

As waters warm or cool even a degree or two, the animal life in the seas moves south or north. Greenlanders depend upon the fishing industry for much of their country's revenue.

Halibut, Norway haddock, capelin, cod, arctic char, and salmon are caught in large quantities. The female lumpfish provide the eggs, or roe, for a tasty caviar. One of Greenland's fastest growing industries is shrimping in the Disko Bay region.

MINERALS

Cryolite was mined for a hundred years. Now the deposits of cryolite have been exhausted. The mine at Ivittuut was the world's chief source of cryolite. This rare mineral is used in the production of aluminum. Although the mine is closed, stockpiles provided an important export until 1985.

A poor quality coal mine on Disko Island operated for many years but it, too, has been closed. On Nuusuaq, a peninsula north of Illulissat, large coal deposits are being studied.

Greenland's only active mine is in West Greenland on Uummannaq Fjord near Maarmorilik. It yields lead, zinc, and some silver. Many other ore deposits have been located including low-grade uranium near Narsaq. The quality does not warrant further mining at the present time.

Five oil exploratory borings were conducted off the west coast of Greenland in 1976-77. The results were negative. Seismic studies indicate there may be deposits in North and East Greenland, but further exploration was discontinued when oil prices dropped. Investigation for oil in Jameson Land continues.

Nuuk, Greenland's capital

Chapter 10

GREENLAND'S RIM

No one lives in Greenland's interior. About 85 percent of the world's largest island is covered with an ice cap. Only Antarctica's ice cap is larger. Most settlements are on the west and southwest coast.

Geographically Greenland is part of North America. Politically it is part of Denmark and therefore Europe.

GREENLAND'S CAPITAL—NUUK

Nuuk, with a population of almost twelve thousand is Greenland's largest town and, as the capital, the seat of the home-rule government. The teacher training college, vocational institute, regional hospital, central library, and Greenland Museum are located here.

A statue of Reverend Hans Egede, the Lutheran missionary who founded the town in 1728, stands on a hill above Our Savior's Lutheran church near the old harbor. Hans Egede's house, built in 1728, is the official residence of Greenland's premier.

Above: Colony Harbor district in Nuuk has many historic homes.
Below: A shopping mall (left); men selling their catch at the fish market (right)

Whaling boats in Sisimiut (note harpoon on boat in foreground)

The new harbor is ice free all year. Coastal and fishing vessels, as well as ships from other countries, use the new port facilities. Many Greenlanders own pleasure craft.

Although many blocks of apartments have been built, there is a housing shortage. A new suburb, Nuusuaq, soon will be Greenland's second largest town.

Up Nuuk Fjord, the remains of Norse homes built over one thousand to seven hundred years ago can be found.

MIDDLE WEST TOWNS

North of the Arctic Circle are Sisimiut (Holsteinsborg in Danish) and Kangerlussuaq airport. Sisimiut is the center of the country's fishing industry. Kangerlussuaq is 120 miles (193 kilometers) up the fjord. The United States air force built a large air base in World War II, and it is still an American military base. Domestic flights and planes from Denmark make this Greenland's most important airport.

Disko Bay

DISKO BAY TOWNS

For at least four thousand years, Inuit hunted seals and whales in Disko Bay. In the seventeenth and eighteenth centuries, whalers from Europe caught whales. Greenlanders still catch a few. Whale, seal meat, and fish are sold at the open air market called "the board."

Ilulissat is located on Jakobshavn Ice Fjord 175 miles (272 kilometers) north of the Arctic Circle. Many tourists come to see the enormous icebergs that calve from the glacier and flow down to the sea. The airport here was opened in 1984.

Shrimping in summer and halibut fishing using dog sleds on the ice in winter are chief occupations. The fishermen chop holes in the ice on frozen Disko Bay or in Jakobshavn Fjord. An ice glider is used to steer the lines under the ice. Each man can catch

Top: The harbor at llulissat
Above: llulissat airport, which opened in 1984
Left: Catching halibut through winter's ice

*A picturesque residential section of Qasigiannguit
with houses perched on a rugged hillside*

between 400 and 600 pounds (181 and 272 kilograms) of halibut
each day.

Other important towns on Disko Bay are Aasiaat (Egedesminde
in Danish), Qasigiannguit (Christianshåb in Danish), and
Qeqertarsuaq (Godhavn in Danish). People in these towns benefit
from fishing and shrimping. Like Ilulissat, there are shrimp and
fish processing factories. Helicopters serve these towns and some
nearby settlements.

THE MIDNIGHT SUN AND POLAR NIGHT

From about May 20 to July 25, people above the Arctic Circle
enjoy the midnight sun. During that time the sun does not set. But
from the beginning of December until about January 12, there is

*Above: Midnight in summer
as it looks at the Arctic Circle
Below: Sorting shrimp for bagging
and export (left), and cutting up whale meat
and blubber at a market for local use*

The aurora borealis as seen from the southern part of Greenland

polar night. On January 13, many towns have a holiday when the sun reappears above the horizon.

In autumn and winter the aurora borealis, or northern lights, are visible. Shimmering curtains of different colors appear in the sky, caused by charged particles from the sun colliding with gases in the atmosphere 35 to 600 miles (56 to 966 kilometers) above the earth near the geomagnetic pole.

SOUTHWEST GREENLAND

The Norse Eastern Settlement, actually on the southwest side of the island, disappeared five hundred years ago. Today, the area is important economically. Fishing and fish processing, seal hunting, sealskin coats, and sheep breeding add to the region and country's economy.

Homes (left) in Narsaq and one of its residents (right)

Southwest Greenland's important towns include Paamiut (Frederikshåb in Danish) north of the Viking Eastern Settlement; Qaqortoq, southern Greenland's important supply center; Nanortalik, where people work at seal hunting; Narsarsuaq, founded in World War II as an American base and now a gateway for planes coming to southern Greenland; and Narsaq, a Greenlandic fishing town that also has a slaughterhouse for sheep. Throughout the summer, many tourists arrive anxious to visit the old Norse ruins.

EAST GREENLAND

There are few settlements on the east coast. The shoreline is rugged and some glaciers come down to the sea. The total population in East Greenland's Ammassalik municipality was 2,768 in 1985. Planes from Reykjavik, Iceland, land at Kulusuk

Left: An Inuit settlement at Kulusuk on the east coast
Right: The DEW Line radar station

where less than 400 persons live. The Inuit, in thirteen small settlements, live much as they have for generations.

Farther north at Illoqqortoormiut there are only five hundred persons. This settlement is just outside the southernmost end of the National Park in northeast Greenland.

The major occupation in the two municipalities is hunting.

THE FAR NORTH

North Greenland's Avanersuaq (in earlier times called the Thule District) municipality has only about eight hundred inhabitants in six settlements. Thule Air Base and the DEW Line, Defense Early Warning system operated by the United States, are located near Inuit settlements.

Camp Century was built in 1960 by the United States Corps of

Left: Camp Century
Right: Thule Air Base on the
northwest coast

Engineers 235 miles (378 kilometers) east of Thule Air Base. For seven years the nuclear-powered city built into the ice cap provided housing and work for 150 people. Many were scientists studying the ice sheet.

CLOSING THE SETTLEMENTS

In 1950, with Greenland's approval, Denmark decided to close small settlements and move the Inuit to the towns where there were hospitals, schools, and improved living standards.

But the program created many problems. Unemployment, lack of sufficient housing, and adjustment to a different culture made the move to the town difficult. Now the home-rule government has decided to discontinue the program.

Each municipality has educational and health facilities to serve the small settlements.

Above: Mummies from the Thule Culture were found in a cave at Qilakitsoq, not far from this rocky shore. Below: The Greenland Museum in Nuuk

Chapter 11

EDUCATION, ARTS, AND CULTURE

THE DISCOVERY OF QILAKITSOQ

In the past fifty years, archaeologists have found many remains of Greenlandic Inuit life. Some date back to 2500 B.C. in far north Peary Land and 2300 B.C. in West Greenland.

The discovery of Thule Culture mummies in a cave at Qilakitsoq across from Uummannaq was especially valuable. In 1978 the Greenland Museum staff brought the five-hundred-year-old mummified bodies of six adults and two children to Nuuk for study. Qilakitsoq was a Thule Eskimo settlement. Ruins of houses have been found also.

The mummy cave revealed how Thule Eskimos dressed, their nutrition, and something about their belief in the magical powers of amulets. Their *kamiks* (boots) were lined with grasses growing in the region. The mummies and their clothing are displayed in the Greenland Museum at Nuuk.

Women making a sealskin cover for a new kayak

INUIT CULTURE

For centuries the Inuit taught their children the basic skills for survival in a harsh climate. They learned the importance of the knowledge of weather and the animals' behavior.

Inuit boys usually began their training in kayaking when they were five to ten years old. The kayak was important in seal hunting. It required great skill to guide a kayak through ice-ridden seas. Old hunters taught the boys how to build a kayak using skins to cover the framework of driftwood or whalebones.

The boys learned to crawl out silently on the ice behind a shield to spear a seal. The seal supplied the family with its basic needs: food, clothing, oil for light and warmth, tools and weapons, and even hides for shelter.

Sled dogs required expert handling to guide them over snow and ice. Dog sleds are used for hunting north of the Arctic Circle in winter today. The hunter still carries a tent on the sled for

This narwhal sinew will be used as thread.

shelter on trips that may last several days. Hunting from snowmobiles or aircraft is prohibited.

Boys were taught whaling and fishing skills. Reindeer, polar bears, foxes, and birds were important sources of food. Survival depended on the hunter's and fisherman's skill.

No less important was the training given the girls. They were taught to prepare sealskins and polar bear and reindeer hides so they could be made into clothing, kamiks, and bed coverings. Sewing the skins and hides into wearing apparel was difficult. The soles and "stockings" of kamiks were made of two layers of skins. Warm fur was on the inside. Grass was inserted between the two layers of the soles for insulation. Hunters today often wear sealskin trousers and boots. For centuries bone needles were used for sewing. The thread was made from sinews.

APPRECIATION FOR THE ENVIRONMENT

The Inuit took only what the family and the dogs could eat. Nothing was wasted. Since they were not farmers, their entire

A dog-sled team at work

food supply came from the sea or from hunting wild game. When the food supply was gone in one area, the people starved or moved on.

Several families lived together to conserve heat in the igloos, tents, or sod houses. Seal oil was used for heating, lighting and cooking.

INUIT ARTS

The Inuit had no written language. Instead, they handed down their history and folklore through stories they shared during the long polar nights.

Wood from Siberia drifted through the Northwest Passage. The Inuit used the driftwood for hunting gear, kayaks, tents, dog sleds, etc. In the old days before they were introduced to Christianity, they also made *tupilaqs*—figures that had supernatural powers and depicted supernatural beings. A display was made of different materials: bones, wood, skin, feathers, etc. The missionaries

Traditional Inuit clothing features intricate handmade designs.

forbade the Inuit to make them and today they are made only for tourists and always only in soapstone, antlers, or tusks.

The women decorated the clothing they made by using different shades of sealskin. Later whalers from other countries traded colored beads as well as tools for blubber and skins. The women used the beads to make festive clothing. The festive national costume with beaded collars and very short pants for the girls and women included colorful kamiks. Lightweight skins with the fur toward the wearer's skin were worn under sealskin pants. White kamiks are for children and young girls, red for those who are married, and dark for older women. These beautiful national costumes that take many hours to sew are handed down from generation to generation.

SPORTS AND RECREATION

The Inuit had few recreational activities. An old tradition, still observed, is to hold a meeting of several communities called an *aasivik*. People set up their tents and enjoy socializing.

In the past, seal ball was a popular sport. The ball was actually a sealskin stuffed with grass.

Popular sports today are the same as in other countries. In towns, boys may play basketball or soccer outdoors until long after midnight during the summer. Skiing, skating, and dog-sled races are activities for winter.

Some towns, like Ilulissat, have sports centers where sports festivals are held. Teams compete in table tennis, volleyball, and badminton.

MUSIC AND DANCE

The drum dance was always popular with the Inuit. Sometimes it was used to settle a dispute. At other times it was danced for pleasure.

The drum was the Inuit's chief musical instrument. Like the tupilaq, the missionaries also forbade the use of the drum as it was closely linked to the Inuits heathen belief.

*Group dancing (left) and a woman
with a drum, once the Inuit's (right)
most important instrument*

In the church, the Inuit learned singing and using the organ and
the piano. From the whalers they learned dances and how to play
the accordion. Today the guitar, the violin, and the accordion are
popular instruments and many old dances and hymns still are in
use.

EDUCATION TODAY

Formal education began when Reverend Hans Egede arrived in
1721. In the beginning, only reading and religious studies were
included. Later arithmetic and writing were added.

In 1905 Denmark passed a law transferring school
administration in Greenland from the church to the Parliament.
Today education and leisure activities are administered by the
Department of Education and Cultural Affairs under the home-
rule government.

All children from ages six to fifteen years old are required to attend school. The first three years are spent in preparatory school. Education continues in the basic, or primary school, from the fourth through ninth class.

If students pass an examination, they can continue for two more years in the secondary school and an additional two years in continuation school. Many students go to Denmark for university-level education.

Greenlandic is the official teaching language. However, since there are not enough Greenlandic-speaking teachers, Danish may be the teaching language also. Students also learn Danish and English.

In the basic, or primary, school, one of the subjects is the handling of hunting firearms.

In sheep-farming areas, parents teach their children at home until they are old enough to attend a boarding school in the nearest settlement.

A public school in Narsaq (left) and preschoolers in their classroom (right)

Ilisimatusarfik is the Greenland University where economics, theology, linguistics, Greenlandic culture, and other areas are studied. The university is developing a complete Greenlandic dictionary.

There are many vocational schools. Courses vary in length from one to three years. They include fish industry training, seamen's and fishermen's school, nautical school, and sheep farmers' training. Special schools train students in building and construction, business, journalism, and metalworking.

The huntsmen's training is offered for both hunters and their wives. Trainees follow experienced hunters to learn animal habits and hunting methods. The wives learn how to prepare skins and furs, flensing, plucking birds, drying meat and fish, and embroidery with colored sealskin.

A mosaic in the National Library tells the story of Greenland.

THE ARTS

The art school in Nuuk offers an eight-month course in stonecutting, graphics, painting, and special artistic endeavors.

When Europeans brought paper, canvas, and other materials to Greenland, the Inuit depicted their daily life, mythology, and nature. There are many young artists. Exhibitions are held frequently, very often in the local museum. In Greenlandic, the word for art is *eqqumiitsuliorneq*.

Among Greenland's finest artists are Jens Kreutzmann, Aron from Kangeq (both from the nineteenth century), Esra Berthelsen, Otto Thomasen, the sculptors and painters Peter Rosing and Hans Lynge, Otto Rosing, painter and author Jens Rosing, soapstone carver Simon Kristoffersen and his family, sculptor Aron Kleist and his daughter Cecilie, and painters Kistat Lund and Akka Høegh.

Theatrical training is offered in Denmark at the private institution, Tukaq. Here Inuit are trained at an international theater school. Artists from the school have returned to Greenland and some of them have formed a theater group called Silamiut that tours in Greenland and abroad.

Chapter 12

INTO THE
TWENTIETH CENTURY

Norsemen established the first permanent settlements and farms beginning at the end of the tenth century. Originally, they had come from Norway. Like the Vikings who settled on Iceland, they traded with Norway. But soon ships from other countries visited Greenland. In 1380, when Norway and Denmark were united, Greenland came under Danish authority.

Although Hans Egede was a Norwegian, he had to seek assistance from the Danish king to go to Greenland in 1721 in search of Norsemen he thought still remained.

CHANGE COMES TO THE GREENLANDERS

From the whalers who came to the island, the Greenlanders obtained materials, tools, and food with which they were previously unfamiliar. However, they continued to fish and hunt seals, whales, and walrus. The polar bear, caribou, and musk-ox were important to their livelihood. But at the newly established settlements, Nuuk, Ilulissat, and other missions and trading posts, they were anxious to trade for European supplies. Changes had come to the Greenlanders (Inuit).

When the population concentrated around the mission stations to obtain tobacco, coffee, cotton cloth, and other items, there was insufficient game to feed so many people. There were no jobs for them. They had no skills other than hunting and fishing. They were unable to adapt to modern civilization so rapidly. In the 1960s, alcoholism became a problem for the people who were idle.

A TRADING MONOPOLY WITH DENMARK

In 1776 a Danish trading monopoly developed. The Royal Greenland Trade Department was established and continued until 1986. One aim was to preserve the native hunting culture. No ships from other countries were to trade in Greenland and disrupt the simple native economy, traditions, and the Danish trade. The population at the time was estimated at 5,800.

WITHOUT CHANGE

Men and women had worn fur garments for warmth. A special garment for women, the *amaat,* was broad enough across the back to carry a baby. The babies wore no clothing but bonnets; they were kept warm against their mothers' bare backs. The hood had a drawstring of sinew to tighten it around the head. Since the women generally wore their hair in top knots, the hood was larger than those of the men.

Reindeer skin was light and warm but it was not durable. Even today, sealers wear polar bear pants for their durability and warmth.

For whale hunting a jumpsuit was worn. A sealskin anorak and trousers, mittens, and kamiks were sewn together to make a

Left: A seal hunter's suit with polar bear pants is on display in the Greenland Museum. Right: Hanging a ship from the ceiling is an age-old custom in Lutheran churches.

watertight suit. The wearer crawled into the suit through the hole in the "stomach" and the drawstring in the hood was pulled around his head. The suit could be slightly inflated to keep the wearer warmer and to help him float if the man fell overboard. This special whale-hunting suit has not been used since the beginning of the twentieth century.

BELIEFS CHANGE

Both men and women wore amulets to be on good terms with higher powers. Often the amulet was a small piece of bone or wood. Since the Eskimos had a great belief in many souls, one for each part of the body, the Christian belief in the soul was understood. The Eskimo believed a soul could be stolen. Their priest was called an *angakoq*.

Today the Lutheran church is the national church in Greenland as it is in Denmark. Hymns are sung in Greenlandic and Danish. There are Inuit ministers serving most of the eighty-five churches and church rooms in Greenland. In 1985 there were a total of twenty-three priests.

Adults and children wearing contemporary dress

MODERN DRESS

All groups of people today that are not completely isolated from the outside world have adopted modern dress. Although the Greenland national costume is worn for special occasions and celebrations, the Inuit have begun to dress the same as the rest of the modern world.

Everyday clothing in towns today is like that in any western country. Blue jeans are popular with young people.

DENMARK RETAINS GREENLAND

In 1814, the union between Norway and Denmark was dissolved. Denmark retained Greenland. In 1931 Norway claimed the uninhabited region in northeast Greenland where Norwegians had traditionally enjoyed hunting and fishing rights. In 1933, the International Court of Justice in The Hague announced that all of Greenland belonged to Denmark. However, Norway was granted hunting rights. In 1965 Norway's hunting and fishing rights were revoked.

The National Conservation Act in 1974 set the boundaries for the National Park. Between 1899 and 1900, wild reindeer were extinct in East Greenland. Concern for the possible extinction of musk-oxen and polar bears hunted by foreigners on the drift ice prompted protection.

SOCIAL CHANGES

In heathen times prior to the colonization, the angakoq was a person of great authority in the Inuit society, and so were other skilled persons in the group: one was an expert in whale hunting, another in trout fishing, a third in reindeer hunting, and so on. Each held authority when his skills were needed. It was a very egalitarian society. Internal disputes were often settled by "drum fights" or " song contests." Sometimes problems could result in blood feuds.

Hinrich Rink studied social decline among the Greenlanders in the 1850s. Rink saw that basic institutions had been destroyed by the Europeans. In 1862 he helped set up a native advisory council.

Originally the small community shared the results of the hunt. Seal and whale meat was distributed communally. In later years, this procedure declined. When the seals disappeared from some regions, the men had to turn to fishing.

THE AIRPLANE "INVADES" GREENLAND

In 1933, Charles and Anne Morrow Lindbergh landed their seaplane in the harbor at Nuuk. They were looking for the best route between the United States and Europe for planes of Pan American Airways. They made several flights over the ice cap surveying the safest route. They reported that a transatlantic route could be flown in summer by way of Greenland and Iceland. Many other pilots flew to Greenland to explore its coastline and the ice cap.

WORLD WAR II

Secretary of State William Seward under President Abraham Lincoln had recommended that the United States buy Greenland as well as Alaska. That did not happen.

When Denmark was occupied by the Nazis in 1940, Greenland needed help from other nations. Greenland's defense fell to the United States, who delivered tons of much-needed food and other supplies. The United States expanded its purchase of Greenland products. Inuit handicrafts were popular with American servicemen stationed in Greenland. Both Canada and the United States opened consulates in Nuuk.

Denmark set up several weather stations. In addition, American air bases were built at Kangerlussuaq, Narsarsuaq, and Ammassalik.

The Germans landed on East Greenland and set up their own weather stations. They broadcast false weather reports, causing several planes to crash on the ice cap when they ran out of gas. Some German weather stations were destroyed by the Northeast Greenland Ice Patrols. Since then four DYE stations (Distant Early Warning—DEW line) have been built and manned by Danes and Americans. These radar stations currently in operation can detect approaching aircraft day or night.

The first elected premier of Greenland, the Reverend Jonathan Motzfeldt

THE GOVERNMENT OF GREENLAND

In 1862 a committee of stewards was appointed for each community. The population in Greenland in 1901 was over eleven thousand. In 1911, popularly elected local and two regional councils gave Greenlanders a voice in their own government. When World War II broke out, the population was still less than twenty thousand.

In 1953 Denmark's constitution was amended giving Greenland two members in its *Folketing,* or Parliament. Greenland was incorporated into the kingdom of Denmark. The population had passed twenty-five thousand. By January 1987, the total population in Greenland was 53,733, of which 9,303 were born outside the country, principally in Denmark.

In 1979, Greenlanders celebrated home rule with a torchlight parade.

HOME RULE

On May 1, 1979 Greenland was granted the right of home rule. The twenty-six-member *Landsting,* legislative assembly, is elected by the people. The Reverend Jonathan Motzfeldt was first elected premier in 1979. There are four political parties in Greenland. The most important are the Siumut (Forward) party and the Atassut (Unity) party. The other two are the Inuit Ataqatigiit (People Who Work Together) party and the Issittup Partia (Polar party).

On January 1, 1986, the Royal Greenland Trade Department turned over most of its functions to the home-rule government. These included banking, postal service, vessels, supermarkets, and processing plants. Greenland Trade Department (KNI) has been formed by the home-rule government.

In 1973 Greenland joined the European Economic Community because of its status as part of Denmark. In 1982 Greenlanders

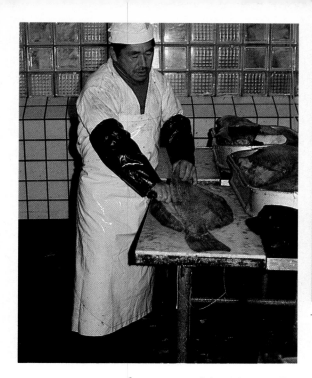

Left: Inside a factory where fish are canned for export
Right: All fruit for Greenlanders' consumption
is imported from other countries.

voted to amend its status. In 1985, Greenland severed its
relationship in the EEC. It provided for control over its 200-
nautical-mile (370-kilometer) fishing limit.

IMPORTS AND EXPORTS

Almost all foodstuffs, dairy products, fuels, and manufactured
goods are imported from Denmark, the United States, and other
countries. Lamb and reindeer meat are used for local consumption
and export. Domesticated reindeer were brought from Norway to
the Nuuk region to provide food, milk, and skins. There is another
herd of about one thousand in southeastern Greenland near
Qaqortoq.

Greenland's principal exports are fish, fish products, fish meal,
and shrimp. Cod and shrimp provide the greatest income. Lamb
and sheep skins and other hides, including seal and fox are
exported also. Now sealskin and other fur garments are made in
Narsaq and Qaqortoq.

A ferry leaving Narsaq harbor

TRANSPORTATION

During the months when the harbors are open, coastal steamers bring supplies and carry people between towns and settlements. Foreign vessels visit the main ports, especially Nuuk.

There are no roads between towns. Trucks, buses, taxis, and private cars use the generally well-maintained streets in the towns. Transportation for travel outside the towns is by ship, helicopter, or small planes. Often schedules are interrupted by fog or snowstorms. And few towns have ice-free harbors in the winter. Of course, there is also the dog sled. Sled dogs are used only by hunters or ice fishermen north of the Arctic Circle. South of the Arctic Circle no sled dogs are permitted on the west coast by law.

The country's first plane was purchased in 1963 and the first helicopter in 1965. For many years, only helicopters could serve

The airport at Narsarsuaq (left) and a shopping district
in Nuuk (right), where you see one of the few buses in Greenland

most of the towns and settlements. Greenlandair has sole right for domestic flights. New airports have been opened, at Nuuk in 1979 and Ilulissat in 1984, and there are sixteen helicopters in service. Many seat twenty-four passengers.

SAS (Scandinavian Airlines) flies regularly from Copenhagen to Kangerlussuaq. First Air has service from Canada via Frobisher Bay to Nuuk. Greenlandair-Iceland Air flies between Reykjavik and Narsarsuaq and Kulusuk and from Iceland to Copenhagen.

In the 1980s, more than fifteen thousand passenger cars, about forty buses, and over twelve hundred trucks, including fire trucks, were registered. These operate only within towns and settlements, since there are no roads connecting the towns.

COMMUNICATION

In 1861, Dr. Hinrich Rink started *Atuagagdliutit*, a newspaper distributed free to Greenlanders monthly. It is published three

This shopping area in Ilulissat provides some of modern life's necessities.

times a week today. In addition, some towns have their own newspapers. *Iluliarmioq* is a local paper published at Ilulissat every second week. Nuuk publishes a weekly, *Sermitsiaq*, which is read throughout the country. Two of the political parties also publish papers.

The central library is in Nuuk. There are public library systems in each of the other seventeen municipalities.

Greenland Broadcasting Service, Kalaallit Nunaata Radioh (KNR) sends out Danish TV programs. Usually news programs sent from Denmark are broadcast three days later. KNR-TV produces a small number of programs, mostly in Greenlandic. The number will be increased with the cooperation of local TV stations. KNR-TV provides the daily TV and radio programs. Every day from Monday to Friday in fifteen minutes and on Sundays in thirty minutes, the local TV stations have their own time to send locally produced programs. Greenland Radio can be heard all over the island. Programs are beamed via the Inuksat satellite.

The hospital at Ilulissat is built on a hill overlooking the town.

In 1986 there were over thirteen thousand telephones. Communication between towns and settlements and other parts of the world is conducted by telephone via satellite, radio telegrams, and telex.

HEALTH SERVICES

Queen Ingrid's Hospital in Nuuk has almost two hundred beds. It is Greenland's main hospital and patients are often flown to it. There are fifteen additional hospitals, all situated in the towns. In 1985, sixty-three doctors were serving the people.

Two of Greenland's major health problems were tuberculosis and alcoholism. In 1960, there were over 250 new cases of tuberculosis with a population of 30,378. In 1985, there were only 16 new cases.

When the Inuit were moved from their small villages to the towns, men who were skilled in hunting and fishing could not

Left: Grønland Hotel in Nuuk   Right: Tourists getting a close-up look at an iceberg

find employment. Alcoholism increased drastically. In the last years, the home rule has tried to fight alcoholism through information, education, better housing, better job possibilities, and higher prices on alcohol. Still it is a major problem.

TOURISM

Nuuk has three hotels. The newest one opened in 1987. Ilulissat now has two. There are small hotels, or seaman's homes, that accommodate tourists in other towns. Greenland hopes to increase its tourism.

Narsarsuaq and the Norse ruins of the Eastern Settlement and Kulusuk on the east coast are frequently visited from Iceland.

The income from tourism will improve the country's economy.

INTO THE FUTURE

Greenland at present has few natural resources to develop other than its fishing and shrimping industry. But under home rule it is

The North Star brightens a bleak landscape

developing its own identity and retaining its culture. The improvement in health services has resulted in a reduction in various illnesses and communicable diseases, and a campaign has been waged to reduce alcoholism. Increased educational opportunities and technical training will enable many Greenlanders to assume positions held by Danes.

Greenlanders warmly welcomed Queen Margrethe II and Prince Henrik of Denmark. They came to Nuuk to join in the festivities in May 1979 when Greenland became autonomous and returned again in 1985.

Just as warmly do Greenlanders welcome those who come to enjoy the stark beauty and historical sites of their country.

MAP KEY

Aappilattoq	B2	Napasoq	D2
Aasiaat (Egedesminde)	C2	Narsaq	D3
Arctic Circle	C1,C2,C3,C4,C5	Narsarsuaq	D3
Atammik	D2	National Park	A3, A4
Atlantic Ocean	D3,D4	National Park	B2
Avigaat	D2	National Park	B4
Baffin Bay	B1	Nuuk (Godthåb)	D2
Camp Century	A2	Nuuk Fjord	D2
Cape Morris Jesup	A2,A3	Nuugaatsiaq	C2
Davis Strait	C2,C3	Nuussuaq	B2
Denmark Strait	C4	Oqaatsut	C2
Disko Bay	C2	Paamiut (Frederikshåb)	D2
Disko Island	C2	Peary Land	A3, A4
Greenland Sea	A5,B5,C5	Qaanaaq (Thule)	B1
Ice Fjord	D3	Qaqortoq (Julianehåb)	D3
Iceland	C4,C5,D4,D5	Qasigiannguit (Christianshåb)	C2
Ikamiut	C2	Qeqertarsuaq	B1
Illorsuit	C2	Qeqertarsuaq (Godhavn)	C2
Ilulissat (Jakobshavn)	C2	Qeqertarsuatsiaat	D2
Isortoq	D3	Qeqertat	B1
Ittoqqortoormiit (Scoresbysund)	C4	Qilakitsoq	D3
Jameson Land	C4	Qorqut	D2
Kangaamiut	D2	Saqqaq	C2
Kangerdlugssuaq	C4	Savissivik	B1
Kangerlussuaq	C2	Siorapaluk	B1
Kangersuatsiaq	B2	Sisimiut (Holsteinsborg)	C2
Kapisillit	D2	Tasiilaq (Ammassalik)	D3
Kullorsuaq	B2	Tasiusaq	B2
Kulusuk	D3	Thule	B1
Kuummiut	C3	Tussaaq	B2
Maarmorilik	C2	Upernavik	B2
Maniitsoq	D2	Uummannaq	C2
Moriusaq	B1	Uummannaq Fjord	C2
Mount Gunnbjørn	C4	Uummannarsuaq (Cape Farewell)	E3
Nanortalik	D3		

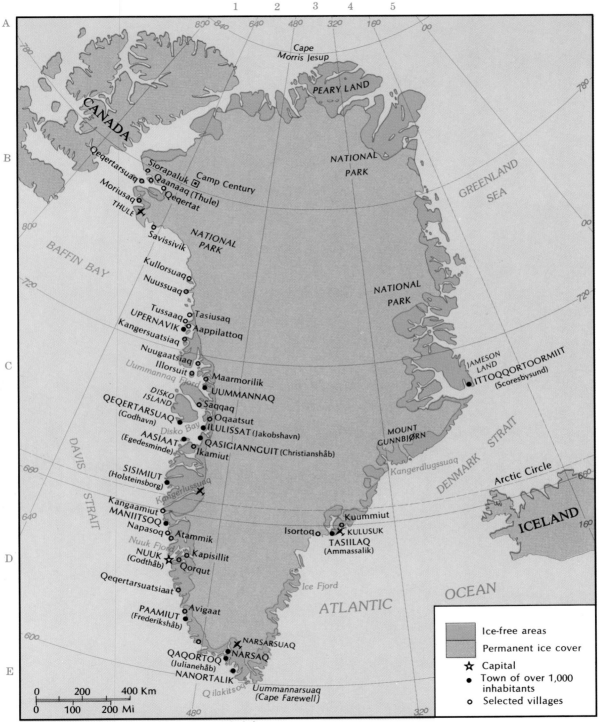

Map prepared by University of Kentucky Cartography Lab

Uummannaq nestles at the foot of a heart-shaped mountain

MINI-FACTS AT A GLANCE

GENERAL INFORMATION

Official Name: Kalaallit Nunaat

Capital: Nuuk (Godthåb in Danish)

Official Language: Greenlandic. Danish is also spoken.

Government: In 1953 a new Danish constitution made Greenland a part of Denmark and gave it two seats in its *Folketing,* or Parliament. In 1979, after a referendum, home rule was accorded to Greenland.

All Greenlanders of 18 years of age or older vote to elect the *Landsting,* a legislative body of 27 members.

Flag: The Greenland flag is half white (top) and half red (bottom), with a circle to the left of center that is white on the bottom and red on the top.

Money: Greenland uses the Danish monetary units of the kroner and the ore — 100 ore equal 1 kroner. Recently the exchange rate has fluctuated between DKr 6 and 7 to one U.S. dollar.

Weights and Measures: Greenland uses the metric system.

Population: Estimated 1988 population — 56,000; 80 percent urban, 20 percent rural

Major Cities:

	1980 census	1987 estimate
Nuuk	9,561	11,209
Sisimiut	4,201	4,716
Ilulissat	3,648	4,135
Aasiaat	3,495	3,231
Qaqortoq	3,056	3,034

The population of Greenland is young: 36 percent are below 20 years old and 7 percent more than 60 years old. The average life expectancy, as of 1985, is 58.5 for males and 66.0 for females.

Religion: Most Greenlanders belong to the Lutheran church, the national church of Greenland. Hymns are sung in Greenlandic and Danish.

GEOGRAPHY

Highest Point: Mount Gunnbjørn, 12,247 ft. (3,733 m)

Lowest Point: Sea level along the coast

Mountains and Terrain: Mountains line the east and west coasts and hold the ice inland like a saucer. The highest, a range of mountains 7,000 ft. (2,134 m), runs along the east coast. Long, deep fjords reach far into both the east and west coasts in complex systems, making for magnificent scenery. Along many parts of the coast the ice sheet that has covered most of Greenland since the Ice Age 100,000 or so years ago fronts directly on the sea.

Climate: The climate of Greenland is bleak and arctic, influenced only slightly in the southwest by the Gulf Stream. Rapid changes, from dazzling sunshine to fierce blizzards, are common. The warmest area is in the fjords on the southwest coast, where the temperature averages 50° F. (10° C) in July and 18° F. (-8° C) in February. The lowest temperature ever measured is -94° F. (-70° C). Snow can, and does, fall in any month.
Average monthly precipitation decreases from 49 in. (124 cm) in the south to 0.6 in. (1.5 cm) in the north.
Most of Greenland has long periods when the sun shines 24 hours a day in summer and not at all in winter. There are periods of "midnight sun" and continuing darkness.

Greatest Distances: North to south: 1,660 mi. (2,670 km)
East to west: 652 mi. (1,050 km)

Coastline: 24,500 mi. (39,427 km), including fjords

Area: 844,019 sq. mi. (2,186,010 km²)

NATURE

Trees and Plant Life: There are few trees on the island of Greenland. Most of the deciduous trees grow in sheltered fjords in the south. Alder, willow, and dwarf arctic birch are fairly prevalent there. The vegetation is represented mainly by tundra types, with heather, birch, willow, and alder scrub together with sedge, cotton grass, and lichen.
The summer is rich in plant life. Winter hay for sheep and many vegetables are grown in the extreme south.

Animals: Sea mammals—seals and whales—were once the main sources of nourishment. Land mammals include: arctic hares, polar bears, musk-oxen, weasels, wild reindeer, white arctic foxes, blue foxes, hares, arctic wolves, ermines, and lemmings.

Birds: The most important sea birds are elders, guillemots, auks, wild geese, ducks, and gulls; land birds include ptarmigans, puffins, grouse, ravens, white-tailed eagles, falcons, snowy owls, snow buntings, and longspurs.

Fish: Salmon and trout are found in the rivers, and cod, halibut, Norway haddock, arctic char, and capelin are important saltwater fish. Shrimping is one of Greenland's fastest growing industries. The abundant marine life off Greenland's coasts is an economic mainstay: seals, fish, white whales, narwhal, and walrus.

EVERYDAY LIFE

Food: Fish, mutton, potatoes, vegetables, and canned foods account for most of the Greenlanders' diet, though seal and whale meat is still important.

Housing: Houses are built of wood and concrete. The bigger towns have a mixture of apartment blocks and smaller houses.

In the settlements the houses are almost exclusively single-family houses. There is an average of 1.1 person per room. Still many houses are overpopulated as there are almost 40 percent of the apartments with 1 to 2 rooms.

Indoor plumbing is normal in most city buildings. It is often lacking in houses in the settlements.

Holidays

> January 1, New Year's Day
> April 14, The Queen's (Denmark) Birthday
> April 20, Prayers Day
> May 12, Ascension Day
> June 5, Danish Constitution Day
> June 15, Valdemar's Day, commemorating victory of King Valdemar's troops in 1219 (when the Danish flag "descended from heaven" over the battlefield)
> June 21, Greenland's National Day
> December 25, Christmas Day

Culture: There is a great effort to preserve the Inuit national culture through language, music, and art. Culture finds most of its expression in Eskimo arts and material effects; such as *tupilaqs,* which were figures depicting supernatural beings that are now made for tourists. National costumes are sewn by hand and passed down from generation to generation.

The art school in Nuuk offers courses in stonecutting, graphics, and painting. Exhibits of local artists are held often.

Theatrical training is offered at a private institution in Denmark—Tukaq. Some Inuit trained there have formed a theater group called Silamiut that tours Greenland and abroad.

Old dances and hymns are still in use today. Popular musical instruments include the guitar, the violin, and the accordion.

Eskimo legends are related to the past. Modern poetry attempts to revive old traditions.

Sports and Recreation: In the old days different sports like wrestling and seal ball were played. Today new sports are popular—primarily football (soccer) in the summer. In the sports centers in towns like Uummannaq, Ilulissat, Aasiaat, Nuuk, Qaqortoq, and other towns, other sports, such as badminton, handball, volleyball, boxing, and tae-kwon-do are popular.

Skiing is very popular in the winter: both cross-country and downhill. Dog races are normally held once in the winter in northern Greenland.

Communication: The press dates back to 1861, when the newspaper *Atuagagdliutit* ("Reading") was started by Dr. Hinrich Rink. It is still published.

The central library is in Nuuk. Other library systems also are found in larger communities.

Broadcasting, which started in 1926, did not become regular until World War II, but it has expanded a great deal and provides a wide range of programming. About 56 percent of the spoken TV programs are in Greenlandic, the reminder in Danish. There are many local TV stations. As of 1987, 66 percent of the radio programs are in Greenlandic. There are local radio stations in Qaqortoq, Nuuk, and Ilulissat.

In 1987 there were over 14,000 telephones, and communication with the world is further facilitated via satellite, radio telegrams, and telex.

Transportation: Air communication has transformed the field of transportation in Greenland. There are no roads between towns. Freight continues to move largely by sea, but mail and passenger traffic are usually airborne.

Dog-drawn sleds are used only by hunters or ice fishermen north of the Arctic Circle.

Flights to and from Greenland use the airports in Kangerlussuaq, Nuuk, and Narsarsuaq on the west coast and Kulusuk on the east coast. Kulusuk is primarily used only for short-distance trips, such as flights from Iceland, as well as a regular commuter flight to and from Kangerlussuaq.

Schools: The educational system is administered by the director of education for

Greenland. Preschool and kindergarten facilities are free. Private kindergarten care can be found also.

Since 1979 education has been compulsory for the first nine years, but it is voluntary for the next four years. Ilisimatusarfik is the Greenland University. There are teacher-training school in Nuuk and occupational and vocational training also is available. Few Greenlanders attend Danish universities.

Health and Welfare: The health service is state (Danish) supported. The central hospital, Queen Ingrid's, is located in Nuuk. There are 15 additional hospitals in other towns. An intensive campaign has nearly eliminated tuberculosis, a leading cause of death in the mid-twentieth century. The fight against alcoholism, a major health problem, continues.

The social welfare service acts in cooperation with the municipal councils. The range of social welfare services is wide. Unemployment is a major problem.

ECONOMY AND INDUSTRY

Chief Products: *Agriculture*—sheep, vegetables
Fishing—cod, halibut, shrimp
Hunting—seals

IMPORTANT DATES

2500 B.C.—Stone Age people come to Greenland

A.D. 9th to 10th century—The Thule Culture people arrive in Greenland.

c 875—Gunnbjørn Ulfsson sights Greenland from a ship that had been driven off course.

982—Eric the Red, a Viking, sails to Greenland from Iceland

1000—Leif Ericsson sails to North America

1261—Greenland votes to join Norway

1389—Norway unites with Denmark; Greenland comes under Danish rule

1400s—Greenland settlers die out

1721—Hans Egede, a Norwegian missionary, establishes mission and trading center

1733 — Moravian missionaries come to Nuuk from Germany

1776 — Royal Greenland Trading company established

1814 — The union between Denmark and Norway ends; Greenland remains with Denmark

1800s and early 1900s — Many Danish scientific expeditions study Greenland

1891-92 — American Lieutenant Robert E. Peary leads several expeditions to Greenland

1909 — Peary claims to have reached the North Pole

1933 — World Court upholds Denmark's claim to all of Greenland against a challenge by Norway

1940 — German troops conquer Denmark

1941 — U.S. takes over defense of Greenland

1951 — U.S.-Danish agreement places Greenland's defense under the North Atlantic Treaty Organization (NATO)

1953 — New Danish constitution changes Greenland from a colony to a province

1966 — Bank of Greenland is established; Danish government begins 10-year, $600 million program to expand Greenland's fishing industry, education system, and housing

1979 — Denmark grants home rule to Greenland

IMPORTANT PEOPLE

Aron from Kangeq (1822-69), artist
Esra Berthelsen (1899-1953), artist
Hans Egede (1686-1758), Norwegian missionary to Eskimos of Greenland
Poul Egede (1708-89), made a Greenlandic dictionary and translated the "Lord's

Prayer'' and the New Testament into Greenlandic

Eric the Red (late 10th century), Viking settler from Iceland who explored Greenland, gave it its name, and settled there

Leif Ericsson (son of Eric the Red), Viking settler in Greenland and adventurer; discovered land he called ''Vinland''

Peter Freuchen (1866-1957), authority on Greenland Eskimos; explorer and ethnologist; with Rasmussen, founded Thule station in northwest Greenland

Akka Høegh (1947-   ), painter

Aron Kleist (1923-   ), sculptor

Cecilie Kleist (1949-   ), sculptor

Jens Kreutzmann (1828-99), artist

Simon Kristoffersen (1933-   ), soapstone carver

Kistat Lund (1944-   ), painter

Hans Lynge (1906-88), sculptor and painter

Lars Møller (1842-1926), Inuit who was editor and printer of *Atuagagdliutit* from 1873 to 1922

Reverend Jonathan Motzfeldt (1938-   ), elected premier in 1979

Fridtjof Nansen (1861-1930), Norwegian explorer, headed first expedition to cross ice fields of Greenland in 1888

Robert Peary (1856-1920), American Arctic explorer; made voyage to northern Greenland in 1891; claimed, now largely disproved, to have reached North Pole in 1909

Knud Rasmussen (1879-1933), authority on Greenland Eskimos, born in Greenland of Eskimo mother; explorer and ethnologist

Hinrich J. Rink (1819-93), scientist and founder of the newspaper *Atuagagdliutit* in 1861

Jens Rosing (1925-   ), painter and author

Peter Rosing (1892-1965), sculptor and painter

Captain William Scoresby (1789-1857), Scottish whaler and explorer who drew first accurate map of Greenland's coast north of the Arctic Circle

Jacob Severin (1691-1753), had the Norwegian-Danish trading monopoly for Greenland from 1734 to 1749

Bishop Jon Smyrill (?-1209), Norwegian bishop who came to Greenland in 1188; bishop of Greenland from 1188-1209

Otto Thomasen (1895-1971), artist

INDEX

Page numbers that appear in boldface type indicate illustrations

About the Author

Emilie Utteg Lepthien earned a BS and an MA degree and a certificate in school administration from Northwestern University. She has worked as an upper grade science and social studies teacher supervisor and a principal of an elementary and upper grade center for twenty years. Ms. Lepthien also has written and narrated science and social studies scripts for the Radio Council of the Chicago Board of Education

Ms. Lepthien was awarded the American Educator's Medal by Freedoms Foundation. She is a member of the Delta Kappa Gamma Society International, Chicago Principals Association and life member of the NEA. She has been a co-author of primary social studies texts for Rand, McNally and Co. and an educational consultant for Encyclopaedia Britannica Films. Ms. Lepthien has written Enchantment of the World books on Australia, Iceland, Ecuador, and the Philippines.